Michael Shea, author, academic, former diplomat and for nine years Press Secretary to The Queen, is now Head of Public Affairs for the massive Anglo-American industrial company, Hanson PLC.

He is married with two teenage daughters and, when not travelling, lives in London and Scotland.

INFLUENCE

How to Make the System Work for You
A Handbook for the Modern Machiavelli

Michael Shea

SPHERE BOOKS LIMITED

A SPHERE BOOK

First published in Great Britain by Century Hutchinson Ltd 1988
Published by Sphere Books Ltd 1989

Printed and bound in Great Britain by
Richard Clay Ltd, Bungay, Suffolk

ISBN 0-7474-0497-6

Sphere Books Ltd
A Division of
Macdonald & Co. (Publishers) Ltd
66/73 Shoe Lane, London EC4P 4AB
A member of Maxwell Pergamon Publishing Corporation plc

To Mona . . . who does

Since my intention is to say something that will prove of practical use to the inquirer, I have thought it proper to represent things as they are in real truth, rather than as they are imagined.

Niccolo Machiavelli

Contents

Preface

> Princes who have achieved great things have been those who have given their word lightly, who have known how to trick men with their cunning, and who, in the end, have overcome those abiding by honest principles.

Niccolo Machiavelli (1469–1527) has always had a bad press. It is generally recognized that Old Nick as a term for the Devil is derived from his name. Considered the archetypal devious diplomat who argued that the end justifies the means, he was in reality a very practical if sceptical man. He stirs up strong views – it is difficult to be impartial about him. Ever the political theorist, Machiavelli is for some the teacher of evil; for others he is a first-class technician, the supreme realist.

His wish was to uphold orderly government and the rule of law rather than, as is often claimed, to enable a corrupt prince to hold on to power. He was above all pragmatic in his advice on how to lead, setting out, to quote Bacon, 'to demonstrate what people are wont to do and not what they ought to do.'

The Prince, along with his other writings, is not a blueprint for this book, but has had a seminal influence on it. Apart from when in pursuit of some obscure quotation, I have used no other books or references.

Very Male-Chauvinist Note

Throughout this book, try as I might, the occasional masculine pronoun has crept in and has been retained for simplicity's sake. But when 'he' or 'him' are used alone, please remember Churchill's remark that, when talking of mankind, he always thought of 'man' as embracing women.

Introduction

All rising to a great place is by a winding stair.
Francis Bacon

There are many books on the market about top people, what they do and how they got there. Although this book will certainly help those who want to reach the summit, it is the first book, so far as I am aware, that is aimed at those who enjoy working behind the scenes, the indispensable right hands of those in positions of apparent power.

This book will demonstrate that:

1 the top is very small;
2 the anterooms on the way to the top are also small;
3 power is never what it seems;
4 responsibility (i.e. formal position) without power is very common;
5 you do not have to be born with influence – you can train yourself to acquire it;
6 there is always a system to be worked.

My approach is to challenge conventional thinking about power and to suggest certain tools which, if handled well, can improve the chances of success of those who would be influential. For top people from all walks of life have individuals – I call them 'influents' – working on them: private secretaries, advisers, speech-writers, gurus, spouses, lovers, hairdressers, chauffeurs. I wish to explain why, in modern society, the alert analyst of decision-making patterns looks first at the president's, prime minister's or tycoon's right-hand man or woman, for that is where the action is. This book, then, is a manual for those who wish to wield influence in business, government and society.

Rule 1

Work the system. Don't let it work you.

Part One

DEFINITIONS

Chapter 1
Power versus Influence

All men are born equal, but quite a few eventually get over it.
Lord Mancroft

Real power, the 'ability to achieve intended effect', to quote Bertrand Russell, rarely exists. Not, at least, in modern democratic society. The freedoms that gave an individual absolute power over others are no more. Despots are out. Social, political and moral constraints act decisively on minister, captain of industry and trade union leader alike. The people whom the headline-writers call 'powerful' are seldom that. In varying degrees they are either in the business of buying obedience or they are influential.

Of course, there are people who, like Tiny Rowland, the chairman of Lonrho, have an aura of power surrounding them. This is partly to do with the awe in which their staff hold them. But this aura stems more from their unfettered ability to take decisions within their own particular empire. Outside that empire they only have influence. Even people who are undeniably powerful have a power that is severely limited.

That is why intelligent and ambitious people no longer seek power as such. Influence – the ability to change events or the minds and decisions of others without necessarily having the formal authority to do so – has replaced power as the goal of the would-be elite.

There are many misconceptions about the nature of titles, positions and authority. For all kinds of reasons we delude ourselves into accepting most public decisions and courses of action as if they were resolved by one person or a single body in authority. We are particularly impressed by titles, even though they do not implicitly imply effectiveness. Phrases such as 'the Prime Minister has decided ...' or 'the Chairman has ruled ...' are commonplace. By using expressions such as 'one of the most powerful men in the country today', we sustain the ludicrous impression that there is still a commodity of effective, limitless power. Such shorthand phrases lead us, the generality, to ignore the subtler reality that lies behind them. However, the world is never as simple as that. Complete freedom to make a decision and to ensure that it is carried out seldom exists in political and social life. How many so-called powerful people cannot even sack their secretaries? Before he got into his stride and into Wapping, the newspaper proprietor Rupert Murdoch could not rid himself of a troublesome but minor journalist on one of his many newspapers, not just because of potential union problems – the man was father of the chapel (i.e. leader of the NUJ branch for that paper) – but also because his brother was influential in the print union of another paper that Murdoch was seeking to buy.

One of the last people in the Western democracies and certainly in the modern governance of the United States to wield real power (according to one biographer, Richard Powers, 'more power, longer than any other political figure in American history') was J. Edgar Hoover, former director of the FBI. His power stemmed partly from the length of time he held the position, from 1924 until 1972, and partly from the nature of the man himself. During the first four decades of his tenure he is considered to have helped America to develop her sense of patriotism and moral order with his resolute belief in right and wrong, sin and punishment, his opposition to change and his rigorous supervision not only of the workings of the FBI but of the American administration as a whole.

Hoover served under eight presidents and it was really only under the last, John F. Kennedy, that he came to be seen as the white supremacist bully that he was, particularly in his opposition to Martin Luther King and the civil rights movement. He and the Kennedys, particularly Bobby, had little in common and, despite the secret intelligence he had gathered on the Kennedy clan, Hoover's power began to be curtailed even within the FBI. Yet even latterly his was, at times, naked power of the most extreme sort. He demonstrated this on numerous occasions when he personally led his 'G-men', trained in the 'machine-gun school of criminology', on shootouts with whoever was currently public enemy number one.

Hoover's power lay, in sum, in the unquestioned acceptance of his total authority in his field by the vast majority, something that Americans would find impossible to countenance today.

What we also sometimes mistake for power is in reality the driving force which many top industrialists possess. But while they can make things tick within their company, they cannot regulate their company's share price. The energy and determination of one person can transform an organization, but at the same time it can weaken it if only one person is doing the thinking or taking the initiatives. Lord Weinstock of GEC is considered by some to be an example of this phenomenon. Until the early eighties he reigned supreme, ever the cold autocrat. But in the aftermath of the Nimrod fiasco and his failed bid for Plessey, his grip appeared to slip – or perhaps he fell into that other trap of great men and became too set in his ways, too inflexible over doing what had always worked well in the past, too sure of himself to be open to the influence of wise counsel. In such circumstances it is almost impossible for someone to regain his reputation of power.

In the real world, therefore, those who are conventionally branded as having the power to take this or that course of action, those who appear to be in the driving seat and with whom the buck may indeed have to stop (particularly if something goes wrong), seldom if ever possess arbitrary freedom of action. The reality is that power, though it still exists, is everywhere in chains. As Harold Macmillan said, 'Power? It's like a Dead Sea fruit, when you achieve it, there is nothing there.'

Traditionally there are considered to be three forms of power: raw physical power or brute force; legal, military or disciplinary power, in which the right to coerce is built into the structure; and financial power, which operates indirectly as a sanction. By way of illustration, let us consider the following example:

Two men are standing on a river bank. Whether they are friends or total strangers, if one tells the other to jump in and swim across, the other may feel little inclination to agree and may stand his ground. If, however, one is much stronger or carries a gun, the likely outcome is that the other will comply. If both are in the army and one is a sergeant and the other is a private soldier, again, the latter will probably do as he is ordered. In the first case the order is enforceable through brute force, and in the second by the threat of a court martial, summary execution for cowardice or whatever. A power relationship, which can also be called a legitimate or *authoritative* relationship, with the ability to coerce or compel obedience, also exists when there is a threat to withhold reward, the financial lever. This argument runs: 'If you do not do what I say I will stop paying you, and you and your wife and children will have to go on the dole (that is, if I can get away with it without being branded by my employees and by the media as a heartless monster).'

Power relationships consequently are executive and are relatively easy to spot. We see the clenched fist or the loaded pistol; we know the power of a drill sergeant; if we have a piper on our payroll, we are entitled to tell him what tunes we want to hear. Power exists wherever formal authority exists although the exercise of that power must take account of the views of others. In other words, the top person's nominal authority is limited, but not extinguished, by his need to influence others and by the ability of others to influence him in return.

Rule 2

Always use the constraints of power.

The relationship between power and influence can be thought of as a spectrum, with power at one end and influence at the other. By and large power is vested in a person's executive function; influence depends on a person's capability to exert persuasion. There is a cut-off area (A in the diagram), which is both qualitative and quantitative, to the left of which is power. In the real world that

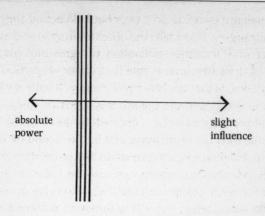

part of the spectrum is very short and depends on the financial or institutional position that the power wielder holds. The band at A is where power and influence overlap or coexist. To the right of that band the much more exciting tool of influence begins, the area where the influent – even if he or she holds an exalted position – lacks the sanction, the means, the capability to *force* through a particular course of action and has instead to turn to other stratagems such as persuasion, suggestion and manipulation to achieve a desired outcome.

Those to the left of A are autocrats, tyrants and the odd remaining dictator, whom some employees may think they have as a boss (they are probably wrong). A recent survey by an American agency, International Security, listed thirty-eight dictators in the world; since the study was undertaken that number has been reduced by at least seven. Even dictators do not have absolute power, however – they frequently have to modify their actions, either in reaction to the people over whom they rule or in anticipation of how the people of other nations will react. The leaders of South Korea in the last decade, for example, have been constrained by massive street demonstrations, US pressure and the desire to host the Olympics. So, unless you are someone extremely special, forget about obtaining untrammelled power. During the American hostage crisis in Iran the Americans had the capability to destroy Iran in a matter of minutes, but President Jimmy Carter was unable to use it. He had the theoretical power; in effect he was powerless.

To the right of A is that much more subtle commodity, influence, the lubricant of the decision-taking process. It can vary from a persuasive whisper in the ruler's ear, which tips the scale in favour of a minor war, to, say, a barely noticed letter to *The Times*, which would be to the far right of the spectrum. As usual, a note of caution is required: influence depends on context and timing. A letter to *The Times* from a bishop was once an important factor in bringing about an abdication.

Influence, in a nutshell, implies the capability to change someone else's behaviour pattern, the decisions that he takes, or otherwise to affect events without actually having the power to do so. It is the art of getting the donkey to run or stop without using the stick. Influence works in two ways. It can be positive or negative, depending on how you want the donkey to act.

A reputation for being influential sharply increases your prominence on the influence spectrum.

Rule 3

You are only influential if you are perceived to be.

Ways of Thinking about Influence

It is well to seem merciful, faithful, humane, sincere, religious, and also to be so; but you must have the mind so disposed that when it is needful to be otherwise you may be able to change to the opposite qualities.

Machiavelli

Corrupt influence, which is itself the perennial spring of all prodigality and of all disorder; which loads us more than millions in debt; which takes away vigour from our arms, wisdom from our councils, and every shadow of authority and credit from the most venerable parts of our constitution.

Edmund Burke

I must follow them. I am their leader.

Bonar Law

The graveyards are full of indispensable men.

Charles de Gaulle

Things are never what they seem. Burke was attacking the breed of faceless adviser who lurks behind the curtains. There he or she is, whispering away in the ear of the ruler of the state or of his cronies at court, in the council chambers and, more excitingly, in the boudoirs. It still goes on.

Burke could equally well have discussed what he might have termed benign influence, and doubtless it would have upset him less. Power, vigour and wisdom lay in 'our councils', but the exercise of that authority was in some way suborned by influence. The first Baron Acton (1834–1902), who is known for the adage 'Power tends to corrupt and absolute power corrupts absolutely' in an age when absolute power was common, went on: 'Great men are almost always bad men even when they exercise influence and not authority. ... There is no worse heresy than that the office sanctifies the holder of it.' Recent events in and around the White House over Irangate certainly go a long way towards giving substance to this and underline the constant need to try to disentangle the exact way in which influence, working on 'authority', produces a particular result.

As long ago as the third century BC, Kautilya, the Indian Machiavelli, whose treatise *Arthasastra* laid down the principles for the preservation and expansion of the Maurya dynasty, recognized the confusion. *Arthasastra*, as highly regarded in India as *The Prince* is in Europe, is essential reading for any student of statecraft. In it Kautilya argues that the influence pattern is less clear than the power relationship because it is seldom direct; rather, by its nature it is elusive and secretive. It becomes even more complex when the person being influenced actually anticipates the wishes of the person attempting to influence him or her.

In the past influence has also been characterized by political theorists as a property or possession, which can be won, lost, appropriated or given away, rather as the nineteenth-century colonial powers acted over the division of Africa. Looked at in this way, the struggle for influence becomes the central purpose of most social and political life. Alternatively, influence has been regarded as *a capability* or reserve that lies dormant unless stirred. However, it cannot exist in a vacuum – a *relationship* is necessary to bring it into being. In fact, all influence requires the existence of a relationship – an interaction between individuals and/or groups.

But an influent's effectiveness is not only dependent on his relationship with the person he is trying to influence. To a large extent it will be circumscribed by a whole set of subordinate relationships. It is no good trying to influence someone unless the people you meet along the line are also prepared to be influenced by you in their turn.

> ### Rule 4
>
> **Identify those you have to influence.**

Influence like power operates in the following spheres: (a) political/authoritative, in which a person is placed in a position of superiority over others; (b) economic/financial, in which influence can be bought or sold; and (c) social, which more or less covers every other human activity.

These categories are not mutually exclusive, as the influence exerted by the economist John Maynard Keynes demonstrates. So impressive and fundamental were his theories that he succeeded in moulding the economic thinking of successive generations all over the world. Even anti-Keynesians were impressed by the vigour of his argument that the classical belief that economies were self-regulating was invalid. But Keynes was no mere theoretician: he was adviser to the Treasury during the First World War and was a British representative at the Treaty of Versailles. During the Second World War he put his advocacy into practice by solving some of the problems of the real world as economic adviser to the Chancellor of the Exchequer. On the international stage he was one of the architects at Bretton Woods of the World Bank and the International Monetary Fund, thereby contributing greatly to post-war reconstruction. In Keynes, status, ideas and his advocacy of them were successfully combined.

Keynes knew and recognized influence. 'Practical men,' he wrote, 'who believe themselves to be quite exempt from any intellectual influences, are usually the slaves of some defunct economist.' How true this is even today. New and radical thinking is not something that one immediately associates with those charged with the fiscal and monetary policies of nations.

Let us now move on to looking at different types of influence. Once we recognize them we can then learn how to use them.

Chapter 2
Types of Influence

Influences on people and decisions come in various forms but there are two basic types: micro-influences and macro-influences.

I experimented with these concepts a decade or so ago with Professor Hugh Stephenson, a former editor of both *The Times, Business News* and the *New Statesman* and now at the Department of Journalism at the City University. We were much into micro- and macro-economics at the time and the pattern seemed to repeat itself in terms of influence relationships.

Micro-influences are direct forms of influence, party to party, one person to another, you to me. The influent may use all his political, moral, social, religious, monetary, commercial, diplomatic, cultural, intellectual, ideological and/or sexual persuasiveness to win his case. Micro-influences, however, do not operate in a vacuum, because there are also macro-influences at work. These are a whole host of indeterminate external pressures which include the world price of oil, world opinion, political stability levels, the state of legislation, the availability of resources, the state of the economy, geographical and communications constraints, the views of the electorate and whether the person you are trying to influence has toothache when you try out your capabilities on him.

On the macro front influence can also be categorized as long-term or transient. Things or people that change man's attitudes or thinking over a long timescale include Britain's weather, Keynes's economic thinking, Darwin's theories, and the French Impressionists. Transient influences are today's good cause (Geldofism, Bransonism, Rantzenism, etc.), hair styles, skirt lengths, 'Dallas' and similar social whims and ephemeral fads.

> ### Rule 5
>
> **Remember that the person you are trying to influence is as subject to the macro-influences of everyday life as anyone else.**

We may think that when we are attempting to influence someone we ourselves remain unchanged. Nonsense. Our target is influencing us in return. For example, he will affect the way in which we present our case. At a more obvious level, we react to and interreact with colleagues, opponents, deputies and friends. We thrive on mutual influence. Some of the great names of industry, for example, actually add to their store of value through a process whereby the talents of one plus one can actually produce three – or four – or five. The sum of the parts, through a process of creative interaction, may well be considerably in excess of the value of each individual constituent. The industrial management company Hanson PLC has been built up through just such a creative partnership between two men, Lord Hanson and Sir Gordon White.

The degree to which someone is influential depends on his or her potential:effective ratio. A father may have great say over what his children do. He may not wish to use it, quite apart from the restraints imposed on him by his desire for domestic harmony, his fear of what the neighbours might say, whether he's tired, what's on television, and so on, he may actually wish to conserve the amount of influence he has in order to keep it in reserve for extreme circumstances. He thus deliberately pushes himself to the right along the power–influence spectrum. By using his influence in moderation (or perhaps by resorting to self-imposed silence) he may engender respect in his children so that, paradoxically, when he decides to act he may actually be farther to the left on the influence spectrum.

As well as the potential:effective ratio there is also the perceived authority factor. This works as follows. A company managing director may wish all his employees to buy and run British cars, but he may decide not to insist on it as he knows there is little likelihood of his being obeyed. The realization that his perceived authority is thus limited and may be opposed, results in the demand not being made. In effect, by anticipating a reaction, he is actually being influenced in his own action. In other words, rather than throwing down a gauntlet that may be picked up, the boss restrains himself and avoids conflict, thereby avoiding possible defeat that would weaken his apparent position. He takes a weak stand now so that he may appear stronger in the future.

Fleet Street management used this strategy for years, but found it did not work in the long run. It took Eddie Shah, followed by Rupert Murdoch, to come along and show that the trade unions' strength was like the emperor's new clothes and that the proprietors' perception of their own abilities could be improved immeasurably.

Let us now look in a little more detail at how influence works in practice.

Influence at Work

We have all seen it happen. The great public figure adjusts his spectacles and shuffles through the briefs on the lectern in front of him. As he leans forward and prepares to speak he is almost masked by a battery of microphones. Television cameras zoom in to focus on him; pencils tap expectantly; shorthand pads flutter; eyes turn attentively. Then, anticlimax, hesitation.

A grey-faced adviser from among the anonymous bunch seated in the row of chairs behind leans forward to whisper in the great man's ear. After a moment or two of consultation, the great man nods and at last begins to speak.

What has happened? Some senior adviser, civil servant or political confidant, totally unknown outside his own peer group, and lacking any power to force the great public figure to take a particular line, has chosen his timing with Machiavellian cunning to cause the words to be altered or amended. Anyone with experience of civil servants of any nationality will have come across this as a daily occurrence.

The first thing that happens when a new minister takes up his office is that all those round him, his private secretaries, his permanent secretary and other officials will, consciously or unconsciously, conspire on how to work him. At the Foreign Office, for example, the skills required for handling the irascible and mercurial George Brown were very different from those needed to handle his cautious successor Michael Stewart, and as different again to manipulate the self-centred David Owen or his successor, 'Mrs Thatcher's glove puppet' (to quote Neil Kinnock), Geoffrey Howe.

Anyone who has regularly to pass the White House in Washington, Downing Street in London or the equivalent government residence in most democratic countries is aware of the continual attempts by groups large and small to influence the decisions of those in nominal power. Petitions, demonstrations, hunger strikes, rent-a-mobs, banners (red is a popular colour) and slogans are their tools. Enormous organizational skills and sums of money may be called into play to mount them. Why then is it that a lone pin-striped figure, bound for the Cabinet Office in Whitehall, striding absentmindedly from lunch at the Athaeneum past the horde of protestors, may have incomparably more influence on the powers-that-be than all those demonstrating outside? What relationship exists between the great public figure and the whisperer in the row behind?

The answer, as Machiavelli said, is that 'when proposals laid out ... look like sure things, even though concealed within them disaster lies, it will be easy to persuade'. In other words, the fortuitous combination of time, place, interpersonal relationships, subject matter and the interplay of various external factors has been astutely manipulated by the influent, and consequently he has affected the perception that the great man has of him, his views and, hence, of what should be done.

One of the most important examples of influence in action is the career of Max Aitken, Lord Beaverbrook, the Canadian-born newspaper proprietor. Always an enigma, he revelled in intrigue. As with many other men of influence, the nature and extent of his persuasion are difficult to gauge for the simple reason he always operated behind closed doors, whispering rather than shouting, concentrating on cultivating those of political standing and financial power. As newspaperman, MP and then peer, Beaverbrook was never interested in formal political activities; his passion was for behind-the-scenes fixing, at which he was adept. His first coup came within a year of his coming to Britain when he played a central role in his friend Bonar Law's elevation to the Conservative Party leadership, while later he helped orchestrate Asquith's downfall. Under Lloyd George's coalition the 'Beaver' served officially as a minister but, more importantly, also as a negotiating intermediary between the representatives of the different parties. Beaverbrook really came into his own as a newspaper proprietor, acquiring the *Daily Express* in 1916. Within a year, as a press lord, he had clearly imprinted his personality and views on a wide readership.

Like other influential men, Beaverbrook did not have it all his own way and, with Churchill, he experienced the wilderness years of the thirties. Then Churchill made him Minister of Aircraft Production in May 1940. In this position he made an incalculable contribution to the war effort through his brilliant propaganda campaign waged both in the pages of his newspaper and in the corridors of Whitehall.

In contemporary times it is not so much press barons (who are tolerated) as civil servants, for example the two Principal Private Secretaries and the Press Secretary, who are perceived to have a huge amount of influence on Mrs Thatcher. Her Cabinet colleagues frequently realize that, against such opposition, they themselves are much farther to the impotent right along the influence spectrum when it comes to decision-taking. The Conservatives do not have a monopoly on influence behind the scenes. One does not have to dig very deep among the Labour leadership to find those that argue that Mrs Kinnock has more than a little effect on her husband, his strategy and his public image. And what could be more natural?

Having got our theory and definitions out of the way, let us now look at the circumstances and setting in which such relationships are put into practice, in other words how to work the system.

Chapter 3
The System

Whatever the hierarchical or management structure of any organization with its normal pyramidical form, there is always a hidden system that bypasses large sections of the 'proper channels' of authority. You have to get to know it.

At the time of Irangate and after the testimony of Colonel Oliver North, the cartoon opposite appeared in a number of American newspapers.

Joking apart, this sort of thing is far from uncommon. A coterie of the managing director plus Bill plus Harry often outweighs the combined organizational structure of the chairman, the board and the sales, production and development directors, etc. Instead of a symmetrical chart set out thus:

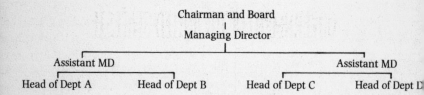

we get the following general triangle of activity:

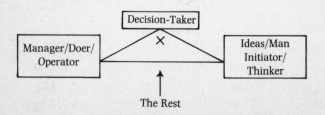

GOVERNMENT OF THE UNITED STATES I

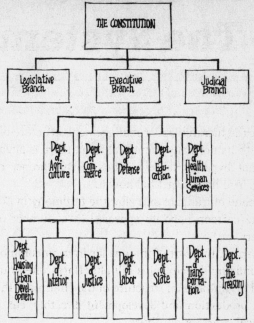

THE CONSTITUTION

Legislative Branch · Executive Branch · Judicial Branch

Dept. of Agriculture · Dept. of Commerce · Dept. of Defense · Dept. of Education · Dept. of Health Human Services

Dept. of Housing Urban Development · Dept. of Interior · Dept. of Justice · Dept. of Labor · Dept. of State · Dept. of Transportation · Dept. of the Treasury

GOVERNMENT OF THE UNITED STATES II

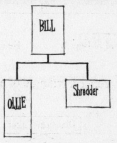

BILL

OLLIE · Shredder

WRIGHT
©1987
MIAMI NEWS

Let us define these individuals.

THE DECISION-TAKER

The decision-taker is the key, the wielder of authority, the holder of the purse strings, the final target. The rest of us depend on him. He is theoretically king, with no superiors, except perhaps the electorate or the shareholders, though he may well have rivals.

When Paul Warneke, President Carter's arms limitation negotiator, was asked whether the 1987 US–Soviet breakthrough on medium-range ballistic missiles would stick, his answer was to ask the fundamental question 'Who's in charge?' It all depended on that. By implication it was *not* the President, but was it Secretary of State Schultz and the State Department or Caspar Weinberger and the Pentagon generals? If the former, the agreement would probably stick. If the latter, the right-wing infighting might well go on for a long time.

> Rule 6
>
> **Always ask of any system who is really in charge.**

THE MANAGER

Any system has to have its manager, the person who actually carries out the work. He reacts, waiting to see what the others are going to do before moving. There is nothing wrong in that. He is well trained, skilled, knowledgeable, but perhaps without much originality – a useful member of the team but unlikely to advance far on his own.

THE THINKER

The thinker is the self-motivated, creative spirit in the triumvirate (though, needless to say, the decision-taker may be highly creative too, just as he may also be a good manager). However, he will need the manager to implement his ideas. For example, Sir Clive Sinclair, although brilliant as an innovator, was unable subsequently to develop his business so effectively. The thinker may even need the manager and the decision-taker to bring it home to him that he has a workable idea in the first place.

The rest are to be tolerated, got round, fought with, or ignored.

PRESSURE POINTS

Follow the devious roads within any system and you will meet left and right turns, constant diversions and apparently insurmountable roadblocks. By the roadside are traffic lights – or Pressure Points – that facilitate or impede the flow or Progress Points that change the direction to right or left or into reverse.

> Rule 7
>
> **Get to know where the Pressure Points and Progress Points are and how and when to press them.**

One of the most important of these points to mark and, if necessary, manipulate is the janitors (Yuppie private secretaries) and *chefs-de-cabinet* who, located at X on the diagram, control access to the target decision-taker. We all know great figures whose doors are protected by a harridan or a smooth-faced ADC who wields authority by controlling access, even if it is only through the appointments diary.

Of course, lesser decision-takers, thinkers and doers have their janitors too, barriers or filters to the centres of activity. How to manipulate and circumvent the janitors is worth a book in itself. Thus, in the Foreign Office the Private Secretary to the Secretary of State can become the filter for all foreign policy decisions and objectives. His handling of his political master can make or break the best efforts of the most senior ambassador. Even the Permanent Under-Secretary will move to second place on the influence grid. We come back to them in Part Five. For the time being, however, note:

Rule 8

Go for who is really important, not who is merely in a title-holding role.

Always ask the following questions about any relationship system – be it in a club, a factory, a Civil Service department, a company, an industry or a state:

- How much real teamwork is there?

- How good is communication (a) upwards, (b) downwards?

- How reliable is the information communicated?

- At what level are decisions made? Which is the level of responsibility?

- What is the pattern of leadership? Are subordinates encouraged to take initiatives? Note the negative (punishment) and the positive (reward) incentives.

- Does this lead to motivation?

- Is achievement recognized?

– How much resistance to change is there?

– Above all, how much of a covert/informal system is there resisting or bypassing the formal system?

At state level, Mahatma Gandhi was a particularly good example of someone who understood the system – in this case the British system for running India. He came to recognize its weaknesses, the longstanding reliance on the rule of law, which he saw would allow his civil disobedience campaign to flourish. With saintly cunning he thus manipulated men and situations in order to convince both the Indian people and the wider world that the issue of Indian independence was a question of morality and nothing to do with the Imperial system at all.

In our own time, the successful takeover bidder will study how things work – how they really work – before making any move. He will note the following unhealthy (for the system) but possibly useful (to himself) indicators:

– Whether there is over-administration – the barbed wire or weighty dross of bureaucracy;

– whether nobody volunteers for anything;

– whether nonconformity is considered bad;

– whether decision-taking is confined to the top (when motivation only comes from the top down it is difficult for new ideas to enter the system);

– whether bright subordinates are not listened to;

– whether competition rather than teamwork is the order of the day, and whether conflicts are covert and office politics rule.

The flatter the structure – that is, the less steep-sided the pyramid – and the fewer levels of management there are, the more successful it is likely to be. As with a piece of machinery, the more pieces there are the more there is to go wrong. If an organization grows too fat, risk-taking and innovation wane. By contrast, a tight organization has less neéd for a 'system' by which to operate.

How the system works is really about two things: decision-making and decision-taking. Let us look at what they involve in the real world.

Chapter 4
Decision-Taking and Decision-Making

Life is conveniently presented as if decisions were taken by individuals in positions of formal authority. But that authority is never as great as it is formal. The president waving to the crowd, the statesman or company director whose signature is needed at the bottom of the document, in short the formal decision-taker, may have made little active contribution to the process by which that decision was actually made.

In the last years of Reagan's presidency the media frequently reported that the President had decided this, given his agreement to that, vetoed the other, when all the evidence suggests that he was only vaguely aware of what was being agreed in his name. Thus, when the buck eventually stopped on his Oval Office desk, he didn't recognize it because he had never seen it before. He was just the figurehead, the mouthpiece. Economic, media, political, personal, social, congressional and administrative micro-influences, along with public opinion, actually forced all the issues and moulded the macro-influences which his increasingly acrimonious White House staffers served up to him.

For similar reasons, any newly elected government soon discovers how limited is its freedom of action to embark on new or original policies. One of the few exceptions is when, now and again, a genuine choice exists and cannot be ignored. Then the minister may actually be forced to *make* as well as to *take* the decision. Otherwise it is easy to prove that a minister is relatively passive, powerless rather than powerful, more a pawn for the influential than a decision-maker in his own right.

Another and much less common exception is when someone outstandingly singleminded is at the top of the tree – a Mrs Thatcher who makes and takes decisions, real decisions, without, if one is to believe her critics, paying much attention to the advice (and less to the views) of those around her. The third Thatcher government may indeed prove George Bernard Shaw's point about rules: 'The only Golden Rule is that there are no golden rules.' Richard Crossman believed that the Prime Minister wields overwhelming power through his or her power of appointment, control of committees, and so on. He would not have seen Mrs Thatcher as an exception.

Decisions have been called the building blocks of life. There is a widespread belief both among theorists and among the public at large that in business, as in government, decisions are taken after a cool analysis of the facts, on the basis of rational thought and calculated argument, carefully balancing the advantages and the disadvantages. This is quite absurd. Most people and organizations are woefully confused in their thinking. Their information system is hopelessly inadequate. Their judgement is clouded by prejudice, ignorance, pride, stubbornness and a host of other factors. They grope and stumble along ill-lit routes to reach conclusions that are often highly detrimental to themselves. Most important of all, decision-makers and -takers almost always allow themselves to reach a decision which is already framed by the language in which the problem has first been defined. In other words, the answer may be all right but the question has been deplorably formulated.

For example, when faced with two options – say, investing in new machinery to improve the product rather than diversifying into a new field, or, in the field of foreign policy, looking at ways of building up the military strength of a Third World country rather than putting all the effort into basic agricultural development – people frequently go for the course of action which led to some previous success, even though the current situation is totally different. History can be a poor tutor or guide. Indeed, a decision that led to failure in the past is not necessarily wrong the second time around; the circumstances may have changed completely.

Of course, we can't all be good decision-takers, as music agent Dick Rowe discovered after he had turned down the offer to represent the Beatles. But when presented with options from which a decision is to be chosen there are nine simple questions we should ask:

1 Who is pushing what? Is the chairman arguing his case because of his finance director's advice or has his wife/mistress/chauffeur been getting at him?
2 If so, what is their motive?
3 Is the decision being framed within the right parameters (e.g. must it really 'cost no more than x or be bigger than y')?
4 Are the alternatives genuine (the 'either you do this or you go bankrupt' argument)? Why can't I take out a bigger loan?
5 Am I being pushed towards the (too) obvious solution?
6 Am I falling into the trap of going by past experience? Circumstances change. What has 'always been the best policy' does not necessarily hold for the present and the future.
7 What's the downside?
8 Where are the biased arguments (including my own)?
9 How many pet theories are there behind what has been proposed?

Finally we should pause and then look at the facts and the possible solutions through a telescope as well as a magnifying glass.

Having seen something of the settings in which and the processes by which decisions are made, let us now turn to how people and organizations set out to manipulate events so that the course of things runs their way.

Part Two
The Ground Rules

Chapter 5
Assessing Your Target

A prudent man must always follow in the footsteps of great men and imitate those who have been outstanding. If his own prowess fails to compare with theirs, at least it has an air of greatness about it.

Machiavelli

There are two basic ways of adding to any skills you may already have in influencing people and events. One is to study how successful people do it and then to follow their example. The other is to sit down and learn some basic techniques. The trouble with the former method (and I give a number of examples later) is that, when good operators are very good, we are so busy listening to what they are saying that we do not always realize what is going on underneath. I have marvelled so many times at David Frost's pre-eminent abilities in negotiating deals (I am not talking about his public, television skills). Everyone is so busy concentrating on his surface glibness, the anecdotes and the jokes, that they do not realize until long after they have got up from the meeting or lunch table what excellent terms he has got for himself or his cause.

Frost, and anyone of his ilk, will begin any attempt to influence a course of action or negotiation (and those involved may not yet realize it is a negotiation) by weighing up his target. It is usually a subconscious process which anyone in business goes through several times a day. That target may be a boss, an equal on the board or even a junior whom you want to persuade to do something he or she does not want to do. The target will be analysed under the following headings:

- His comparative institutional status;
- His ability to influence others (does the head of programming actually carry any weight?);
- His educational, cultural and financial standing (does he need the money?);
- His social standing (will he be attracted by the prospect of a knighthood if he takes on the chairmanship of the quango?);
- His moral strength (how honest is he?);
- What his resources and allies are like (the 'web of friendship' factor);
- What his anxieties are (the fear of redundancy, etc.);
- His relative strength of will (some of the most successful take-over battles have been more to do with this than with money);
- How he is perceived (his reputation) in relation to all the above by colleagues/the media/the world at large.

You should ask yourself:

- Is he a risk-taker?
- Is he ruthless?
- Is he sincere?
- Is he a bluffer?
- Is he subject to stress (see below)?
- Will he be easily duped?
- Is he susceptible to flattery? (Show me a successful person who isn't.)

Rule 9

Prepare a mental dossier on your target before you begin.

There are many other things to look out for in your target. If he is opinionated or likes to hear himself talk or has something important to say, it is better to keep quiet. The acolytes and employees of the mercurial British newspaper tycoon Robert Maxwell have to learn this skill rather quickly or they don't stay around for long.

From this we learn the three ground rules of listening:

1 It takes a wise man (or a survivor) to make a good listener.
2 Great things (like surviving) can be achieved by being silent at the right time.
3 Listen actively; be seen to listen.

Another lesson to be drawn from assessing the target is the ability to recognize when you are likely to be beaten. The American union boss Jimmy Hoffa's views were always expressed lucidly and to the point: 'I may have my faults,' he said, 'but being wrong ain't one of them.' People like Sir Gordon White have got where they are by watching the downside and not going after companies that they know they cannot get.

Similarly, beware the 'I didn't think of it so I'm against it' type, a common enough fault among many business leaders. On the other hand, Machiavelli himself warns us: 'Humility is not only no help, but a hindrance, especially when used in dealing with arrogant men.' Very true in the right circumstances. Jeffrey Archer would not have been able to bounce back from bankruptcy and other misfortunes if he had been humble. As someone once said of him, 'He has overcome his shyness.'

A pre-eminent assessor of targets and situations is Lord Goodman, described by many as the most influential man in Britain today. He provoked me into coming up with one of the most telling rules of decision-making:

> ## Rule 10
>
> **Don't rush to judgement. Always take time for a second look.**

In a recent profile in *The Times* Goodman was given the title 'the

universal fixer'. He has been involved with many national institutions – from the British Council to the Royal Opera House. He has
served on royal commissions, on numerous quangos, was chairman
of the Newspaper Publishers' Association and Master of University
College, Oxford. He was widely regarded as the Arts Council's most
successful chairman.

Harold Wilson summed up Goodman thus: 'He has helped the
system to work when it wasn't working.' The key to his influence
is that he is 'ingenious in finding solutions and quick at it.' He
possesses great powers of persuasion and, because of his discretion,
has few real enemies. He is an outstanding example of an influence
broker. Although sympathetic to the Labour Party he was never a
party member, and this enabled him to form friendships and contacts
with important individuals right across the political spectrum. That
is why, while I was a desk officer in the Foreign and Commonwealth
Office, Goodman was asked by both Heath and Wilson to help bring
about a settlement in Rhodesia. His attempts failed but those arch
political rivals both continued to employ him because, as Heath
said, Goodman 'knew all the people and did all the work', the
supreme tactician in every way.

From the experience of having seen Lord Goodman at work comes
the following:

Rule 11

**If you can influence the top you can be as
influential as the top.**

Chapter 6
Self-presentation

One man that has a mind and knows it can always beat ten men who haven't and don't.

George Bernard Shaw

To be influential you have to know what your core objectives are. You have to ask yourself, 'What do I want and where am I going?' Are you seeking rewards or satisfactions? If so, what are they? Are you after:

- a formal position that is assumed to be 'power' (i.e. the top job)?
- influence for its own sake/something less than the top job/to be the 'right-hand man'?
- propagating some model/making people adopt your way of doing things?
- safeguarding your existing position (often by opposing any change)?
- obtaining a specific decision?
- money, more money, or things, like property and diamonds, that you don't have?
- less immediately quantifiable goals (peace, sex, leisure, and so on)?

You may indeed want several of the above, and you will probably have further, secondary goals as well, some of which may be incompatible, like making sure that you do not upset your spouse. You also have to decide whether you want to persuade or dissuade your decision-taker or merely to reinforce or modify his course of action. You may not want, for a variety of reasons, to go for the obvious rewards. Even highly successful and motivated entrepreneurs will opt for, say, influence for its own sake rather than for hard cash, or for a reliable and stimulating personal relationship rather than increased profits.

You may have to disguise your main intention. It is not always a good idea to lay all your cards on the table at once. Don't breeze into the chairman or the minister and tell him/her how to do things. Be as subtle as you are when you say to your secretary, 'Would you mind very much making me a cup of coffee?' rather than 'Make me a cup of coffee, now!'

The rules here are:

- Suggest to the decision-taker that he has freedom of choice.
- Make it clear that he can reject your view and do something totally different.
- But since a person's greatest desire is to feel important, point out that he will be widely respected if he does as you suggest.

There is, of course, great virtue in knowing what you want and in setting out to get it in a totally dedicated and singleminded way. But few of us have the style or resolution, unlike, for example, the Duchess of Norfolk in her campaign to raise funds for her hospices. A lady who is strongly averse to taking no for an answer, she uses every contact and influence in her large armoury to that worthwhile end. She is a one-woman case study of what much of this book is about. Which leads to:

> **Rule 12**
>
> **Single objectives work best. A multiplicity dilutes your chance of success.**

WHAT YOU SAY YOU WANT

It is of the utmost importance that you should consider what is to be done rather than what is to be said. It will be easy, when you have arrived at a decision, to accommodate words to acts.

Machiavelli

What you want and what you say you want, even if you are totally honest with yourself and others, are likely to differ. Machiavelli is suggesting that you decide what you want first, then explain. Whether you are actually in pursuit of kudos, the lusts of the flesh or a large backhander, what you say that you want should always be well larded with what are known as 'full-stop words'. Politicians use them all the time, as do business executives engaged in takeover bids or property developers and conservationists when they join battle over some piece of land. Try arguing against those who use them: you will soon see why they are called 'full-stop words'. They go beyond mere macro-influences and include such heroic concepts as the National Interest, Morality, Justice, Liberty, Honesty, Independence, National Security, Peace, Self-determination, Motherhood, Fair Play, the General Good, Humanity, Stability, Harmony, Decency and Progress.

In the same context note also the prevalence of the 'as is well known' syndrome and the 'it is self-explanatory' argument. When confronted with such phrases always ask who said so first and why.

If you are going to use such terms, always be consistent. Machiavelli himself, quoting a contemporary proverb, warned of 'the man who is of a different opinion in the marketplace from what he is in the Palace.' You can, of course, get away with saying different things in different surroundings provided you choose your audience well and so long as the masses, for example, do not get to know what is really being planned and said in the antechambers of authority. But there is a danger in believing that the public is swayed more by what people say than by policies. Before the 1987 British general election many political pollsters argued that the image of the party leaders and their style, rather than their advocacy of particular causes, would win the day. In the end, despite Neil Kinnock's much vaunted 'image' campaign, it was the Thatcher policies, *not* her image, that won.

However, from all the evidence, it is not just in Britain that style and presentation, what you say and how you say it – preferably simply and directly – frequently produce the desired results. The American presidential style of campaigning runs along the lines of

'My fellow Americans, believe me, all I want for us is Peace, and Security, and Prosperity, and Liberty, and Justice, and Equality, and . . . .' In fact, that sort of patter is as old as the hills and can be found in democracies and dictatorships throughout the world.

DEFINING YOURSELF

You know what you want or think you want. But, in order to achieve it, you have to recognize what sort of person you are.

There are two basic types of successful man or woman: the self-motivators and the reactors. The latter are by no means less successful than the former, so do not belittle yourself if you think you are in this category. However, the former will be a lot better at spotting and using the talents of the latter.

So, once you have defined yourself as a creator or a reactor, you can decide how best to move on to the next stage.

FIRST STEPS IN SELF-EDUCATION

> The mistakes are all out there waiting to be made.
> *Chess Grandmaster Tartakower*

You know who you are and what your aims are. What are you going to do about it? The first step is to learn to present yourself in the best possible light.

You have got to appeal to people, or at least your ideas have to. You have to make sure that you are what your target decision-taker wants. If you are not, then either you have to change yourself or you have got to change him – adapting, as any economist will tell you, the demand to match your supply.

The American writer and exponent of The New Journalism, Tom Wolfe, has analysed and exposed the difference between status and posturing with brilliant acuity, but most people cannot separate style from substance. That is why many public figures, from Mrs Thatcher to would-be mega-businessmen, take elocution lessons. They all realize that how you speak, how you pronounce words, as well as the accent you were reared with, not only classifies you but also affects other people's perception of your status and potential influence.

Do some market research to establish what your target decision-maker wants, then create for yourself what sales managers call 'hidden demand', which means a demand for your services that did not exist before. Develop an aura which says: 'You really can't do without me.'

Despite de Gaulle's adage about the graveyards being full of 'indispensable men', make yourself indispensable. Marlborough's lieutenant, the 1st Earl of Cadogan, was known as the 'maid of work' because of the variety of duties, both important and menial, he undertook. He had a great personal influence both on his leader and on world events for the simple reason that Marlborough and his peers could not do without him. A common term of abuse in contemporary political and commercial circles is to describe someone as a 'gopher' (go for this, go for that). Don't despise gophers. Like the Earl of Cadogan, they make things tick, and they frequently take over from those for whom they once gophered. Which leads us to:

Rule 13

Unless you can hold centre-stage when you choose to, you will not get recognition.

Here are ten general rules to help you improve the way you present yourself. We shall deal with more specific ones – for example, when faced with the prospect of a television interview – at a later stage.

1 Optimism is a necessary precursor of success. Show it.
2 Look interested. Look alert. Even try to be amusing. Then you will be interesting.

3 Keep working up new ideas and strategies. Self-motivation can be fun – and rewarding.
4 Keep reviewing those strategies.
5 Know when to stop. Know when to cut your losses.
6 Know when to listen. Recognize when being silent can be more rewarding than holding centre stage.
7 Be ready for the quantum leap when it presents itself.
8 Recognize that there is usually a middle way between preaching revolution and crying sedition.
9 Appearances count. Some people immediately categorize you by your tie knot or skirt length. Dressing for success pays off.
10 Get yourself perceived as influential. A reputation for this is almost as good as the real thing.

There are lots of other tips floating around for you to add to your own achiever's manual, like the statistical fact (in the USA at any rate) that thin executives get farther than fat ones. Clichés such as 'Ambition is good for you (and you shouldn't feel guilty about it)' also seem to work.

But do not push too hard. One way of not getting there is to offer too much criticism too freely. Some people can take it, others cannot. The latter are put on the defensive, their pride is hurt and, if criticism is delivered in front of an audience (bad enough in front of a peer group, worse in front of underlings), the damage to the victim's sense of self-importance will lead to resentment and hostility.

A little dissent sometimes does not come amiss. As Harold Macmillan said, 'By all means rebel, but only on one issue at a time.' Dissent suggests an alive and independent mind. However, it must *only* suggest that.

It is quite remarkable how man's natural propensity for sloth constantly reasserts itself. You must keep looking for a focal point for your perceived abilities. Never forget the 'I'm here' factor or the 'You need me' appeal. This may sound rather pushy but, done carefully, it can be both seemly and effective.

AN A-TO-A CHECKLIST FOR THE INFLUENT

Aims   Know them and how and when to aim at them.

Appointments   Keep them. Don't keep people waiting.

Aggression   Beware of showing too much.

Availability   If you always are, it helps.

Appreciation   Give praise when it is due.

Arrogance   A little does no harm in the right circumstances.

Apparatchiks   Watch them: they are the 'no'-men of any organization. They have to be appeased or neutralized.

Assurance   (Perhaps reassurance.) The 'Do this and you'll be OK' approach.

Allies   You can never have too many.

Articulateness   Should be developed if lacking.

Access   To the target decision-taker is crucial.

Audience   Catch and hold.

Acting   Play the part required, from determined to nonchalant.

Assessment   Weigh up before acting.

Advertisement   (Self-advertisement, that is.) This is the 'I'm here, you need me' factor.

Chapter 7
Assessing the Opposition

Know the enemy and know yourself, and you can fight a hundred battles with no danger of defeat.

The Chinese philosopher Sun Zi, quoted by Chairman Mao

Having weighed up yourself and your target, the next stage is to identify who else is around who can or may influence your decision-taker. Apart from your peer group and your colleagues, your superiors, your deputies and your deputies' deputies (tomorrow's men and women), beware also the secretary, the personal assistant, the spouse, the lover, the chauffeur, 'friends', the taxi driver who just happened to bring the target decision-taker in from the airport, (there is nothing much you can do about the 'chap I just met, salt-of-the-earth, primitive but perceptive' influence, except hope it will last no longer than the encounter itself did), the image-maker, the guru, and the *eminence grise*.

We will come back to the last three later. The other dangerous (because it is inanimate) competition comes from the decision-taker's access to and use of other information sources. For example:

- he reads the *Financial Times*;
- he plays with his data bank before going to bed every night;
- he has a team of dedicated (young, enthusiastic, committed) research assistants who fill his briefcase and in-trays with 'informational research'.

All that is bad news. The decision-taker will certainly be better equipped, as a result, to weigh the various competing sources of influence. He may even enjoy himself by creating conflicts between you and the other sources in order to get the results he wants. You have to employ the devices in this book very carefully to neutralize as many channels of likely contrary influence as possible.

This was the method of the French statesman, the Duc de Richelieu, who, for many years, was virtual ruler of France. He set about creating a centralized autocracy for King Louis XIII, with Louis as the figurehead, but with Richelieu himself holding all the reins. While perhaps not quite the Machiavellian practitioner of *realpolitik* that he is often considered to be, Richelieu seldom felt himself inhibited by moral or religious constraints. Ruthless and shrewd, he thwarted plot after plot to oust him: the great conspirator identified, then got to understand his opponents. Having analysed his prey, he was adept at using them to his advantage. In today's world knowing your enemy remains just as important. There are few takeover bids in the City of London or on Wall Street in which the opposing team do not run a psychological screening or profile of their main opponents to find out what their weak points are.

There are many methods of playing the opposition. Much the best way of getting your point of view accepted is to point up other people's mistakes. They are bound to make them. And in this game two wrongs by the opposition make a right for you. Perhaps the opposition does not make mistakes. There are ways they can be helped to. And others can be made to notice them. We shall come back to this.

CREATING OPPOSITION

Many, therefore, believe that when he has the chance, an able prince should cunningly foster some opposition to himself so that by overcoming it he can enhance his own stature.

Machiavelli

Fostering opposition is a useful little device: a perceived opponent is a good means of rallying support among your colleagues or bracing your target decision-taker when he/she feels like wavering. However, guard against the danger (which nations succumb to all the time) of paying more attention to your adversaries than to your allies. Also try not to create unnecessary enemies by, for example, abandoning those on whose backs you have climbed to get where you are.

NEUTRALS AND THE DANGERS OF TRADITIONAL BELIEFS

> A neutral is bound to be hated by those who lose, and despised by those who win.
>
> *Machiavelli*

Clear-cut opponents are dangerous but are usually visible and straightforward; neutrals and fence-sitters can be both a nuisance and tricky to handle. And the most important fence-sitter may be the decision-taker himself. He may wish to remain boringly neutral. He may resist your most carefully worded blandishments. He may have strength of character. He may indeed have views of his own. He may even try to influence you in return, either directly or through third parties. You have to judge how much to push your persuasive attempts when the response is, 'Stop burbling on, Jones, or you're for the chop.' If you are working for an autocrat like Sir James Goldsmith, Robert Maxwell or Rupert Murdoch, you may be foolhardy enough to try to change his decisions, but you are more likely to end up saying, 'OK, sir. You're quite right. I agree, of course. What a good thought. Just right. I'm with you all the way.'

Neutrals (decision-takers or opponents in disguise) take cover by appealing to tradition – 'We have always believed/acted in this way' (you can use it too) – or they may resort to citing precedents. Those who always say, 'OK, get out the file and see what we did last time,' are always difficult to budge. This is usually a sign of weakness. As John Kenneth Galbraith explained: 'Such buttressing of weak bargaining positions becomes, as a result, one of the most important of the functions of government.'

It is a folly none the less to ignore traditional views, the 'we've always done it this way' line. Thus Lord Whitelaw and his considerable influence in the modern Conservative Party in Britain. As the last of the so-called Tory grandees, he is perceived to be the defender of the soul of the party, a wise counsel but able to wield a big stick when he has to. In the past he was not above making an indiscreet comment to a journalist so that the resultant leak, from an 'impeccable government source', would frighten a wayward policy back onto the traditional rails.

Rule 14

Faced with an entrenched or neutral position, remember there are always two ways around it.

Chapter 8
Time and Tide

In communicating to good effect, time, place and the level you work at are all crucial. Of these three, timing is the most important factor of all. If your target is a fool, you may win when he is tired, drunk, jet-lagged, on the way to lunch (or on the way back), late for a secret liaison, up against a deadline, just about to address a meeting or when you have just done him a favour.

On the other hand, these may be quite the wrong times if your target is clever. Then you must get to him when he is thinking well, is not flapping, is likely to remember what you have just said and is ready to take decisions.

By contrast, the successful man or woman never lets his/her opponents find him/her in any of the above situations. It is here that the art of selecting a good secretary lies: find someone who knows when not to put calls through to you (and that does not just mean when you are on a low). It is probably the best investment any manipulator of whatever level can ever make.

A good secretary will recognize when you are firing on all cylinders, having a domestic crisis, need support, need to be left alone, need a stiff whisky, need a haircut or to lose weight to increase your morale.

But there is an additional overriding art to timing which is sometimes known as *primacy* – the 'getting in first' effect. There is nothing to beat it. My experience is that strong, favourable arguments put forward at the very beginning, for example, in a debate, are harder to knock down later. All in all, bad timing can ruin the best case. In a takeover bid, the first serious offer is always harder to resist. It comes as a surprise – the opposition are unprepared.

The counterblast may, of course, succeed in the long run, but only after the initial advantage has been overcome.

You will seldom see an immediate effect. There will always be a response lag which will be in inverse proportion to the amount of oomph you put behind your game play. Sometimes you will have to wait a couple of minutes while your victim balances out the options in his mind. At other times you may have to wait a year or so while your drips of advice (I call it 'creeping influence') are gradually absorbed.

It is axiomatic that creating deadlines is a great way to get people to come to conclusions. Rupert Murdoch did this when he gave the government a mere matter of hours to agree to his purchase of the *Today* newspaper not going before the Monopolies Commission. The less time you give people, as Murdoch knows, the less time the opposition has to marshal its case. Those most opposed to the *Today* purchase had hardly begun to mount their attack because they did not believe the government would give in. The government did, and Murdoch acquired another paper.

You can learn a lot from timing strategy like this, and just as much when things go the other way. General Haig got his timing and his presentation wrong after President Reagan had been shot. Sir Freddy Laker got his timing wrong in his battle with the major airlines, although his ideas and policies were excellent so far as the travelling public were concerned.

John Foster Dulles, by contrast, developed timing to an art form. The word 'brinkmanship' was more or less invented for him. Again and again he would push the Russians to the limit, almost to the point of war. He usually got it right – as far as he was concerned, that is. The rest of the world was not too sure.

SUBJECT, LEVEL AND LOCATION

If people in general perceive you to be influential in one respect, some of them (and even you) may think you have standing in other areas as well. But if, for example, you are known to be influential in assessing stock market trends, do not be surprised if they ignore your advice on which horse to back in the 3.30.

Depending on the subject, the degree of influence you have will differ vastly. And the degree of access you have will also vary. It is widely believed that Lord King of British Airways has the ear of the Prime Minister Mrs Thatcher. But his influence, although clearly personal, is in no way universal and he has had to moderate his position from time to time in order to continue to be listened to.

Choose the right level to operate at. Do not aim too high. The top man may not actually be the decision-maker. As a general rule it is better to go for the minister's private secretary than for the minister, though not, of course, if the former is likely to stifle your views for his/her own ends.

Rule 15

Choose the right level. Never put an important case to a vice-president. In-between people are in between.

This is particularly true in the United States where those who have outlived their usefulness in any organization are appointed vice-president. The British, with the model of the House of Lords to go on, find meaningless yet statusful titles – non-executive chairman, consultant editor-in-chief and so on – for their in-house pensioners' rest scheme.

Finally, make sure you choose the right location. Where you make your sales pitch can be crucial. Consider the following options: in the boardroom, at the club, over lunch/dinner at a small corner table, on the fourteenth tee, in the loo.

Probably the best general advice is to act on your own territory, if you possibly can. This is known as the territorial imperative. Away games are harder to win.

Rule 16

Use territorial imperative: act on your own ground.

Chapter 9
Communicating

You have all the participants lined up. You know everyone's respective strengths and weaknesses. Now all you have to do is get your message through. Many deals have been aborted simply because they have been sold badly. So much depends on the environment in which you are working. Any business or government institution has its shorthand system of communications, the nods-and-winks approach, otherwise known as Company Chinese. In any society, indeed in relations within your own family, there are usually shorthand methods of passing messages in a much simplified form, including what is termed body language. A clenched fist is a threat or a signal of a threat, just as a woman's discreet wink can indicate some more exciting possibility. As Desmond Morris has pointed out, there are many very subtle methods of signalling, from the way you sit when you are talking to how many buttons a woman has undone on her blouse.

In other words, when people are making decisions they use not just words but also signals, often unconsciously, for certain strategic purposes. You have to use your eyes as well as your ears to get certain messages across as well as to receive them. The sentence 'I don't think we ought to, do you?' can be 'read' in several different ways. It can be transformed by a scowl, a shrug or a come-hither look. Try saying it to yourself out loud. The general ambience, the tone of voice and so much else can give the receiver of a message a gut feeling about what is *actually* meant.

Communicating both with words and with body language is all about practising empathy with your interlocutor. You speak and act to establish yourself as an authority figure who possesses knowledge, experience, realism, expertise, self-control, self-detachment, energy, dynamism, integrity, dependability, and the ability to get and hold attention.

A key example of someone apparently possessing all these qualities, and consequently perceived to be highly influential, is the veteran American television journalist Walter Cronkite. 'I don't believe the news unless Walter Cronkite tells it', is an old joke, but one that is remarkably close to the truth. Cronkite, in presenting the evening news for CBS, became the model of the honest, objective professional, a figure seldom rivalled in the history of television. Americans still believe he gives them the truth and nothing but the truth. But Cronkite himself says, 'I give the people the news; I don't tell them how to think.' And again, 'I am a news presenter, a news broadcaster, an anchorman, a managing editor, not a commentator or analyst.'

Some argue that there is no such thing as objective, unbiased reporting and that the way you present your facts reflects and endorses your opinions. (We shall come on to 'facts' later.) But the key to Cronkite's influence, paradoxically, is the very fact that he does not seem to seek to influence his audience.

There is no one quite like Cronkite in the British media. The Burnets and Dimblebys have their following and doubtless win votes with their differing styles. But British television is closely scrutinized by the political parties and anything smacking of undue influence is immediately suppressed.

The important rules of communication for you, the would-be decision-maker are:

- Always to try to influence any constraints and play on any susceptibilities to which the decision-taker is subject. If he likes to laugh, make him laugh.
- Never worry, as Disraeli said, about being 'a burglar of other people's intellect'. There is no copyright on good (or bad) ideas.
- Always get across the potential rewards and penalties of not following your advice.
- Create a 'perceived community of interest' with the decision-taker, stressing any common ambitions.

   – Go for self-fulfilling prophesies, remembering that in communicating 'a little lie sometimes saves a lot of explanation'.

Make sure you use what you are communicating to work for you. Dr Bernard Donoughue (now Lord Donoughue), one of Harold Wilson's main advisers between 1974 and 1979, has been likened to an Elizabethan courtier in this respect. His great skill was trading information, bartering what he knew in exchange for what others knew, building up, in the process, a network of confidants. He thus created a reputation for being in the know and having an influence which, even by his own admission, he did not always have.

Communicating in order to influence is, after all, not too dissimilar to salesmanship. That is why a business or a political party that wants to sell some commodity or idea to you will choose a person who appears to have Cronkite-type integrity to present its case.

The salesman does not have the power to force anyone to make a purchase. He has to get across a description of the product, to build up its appeal so that he does not have to sell it to you so much as you want to buy it from him. We can all see why some sales pitches, like party political broadcasts, succeed, while others, again like party political broadcasts, drive off more customers or electors than they gain.

Integrity does not always work, however. A lot of people liked Adlai Stevenson but did not vote for him. In Britain, the two Davids, Steel and Owen, topped many a poll for trustability and likability but did not win many seats for the Alliance.

The basic sales argument is: Buy this product (or course of action) because:

   – realize it or not, you need it (a new three-piece suit or 'Tory Party values').
   – you cannot do without it (a life insurance policy or 'Labour's social conscience').
   – you want to keep up with the neighbours (and they all have Porsches and swimming pools *and* vote for the Alliance).
   – you want to improve your lot.
   – you have got into the habit.

Influence peddling is very like selling insurance. You sell yourself, then you sell your product. A degree of honesty is required since a good salesman wants the customer to come back. He has his eyes on the sale after next. His success rests on his credibility and the passion behind the message: 'What will happen if X befalls you and you don't have it?' or 'What will happen to your dependants if one day . . .?'

Even though it costs a great deal, the client will probably buy, through a mix of caution and fear of the consequences of *not* doing so.

Hence the influence of Sir William Beveridge, whose report at the height of the Second World War in 1942 had, arguably, more effect than any other government paper before or since. It was, after all, to lead to the creation of the post-war welfare state. Beveridge knew and understood that it was influence alone that he possessed. He put forward a message that suited the time, analysing its effect in his autobiography *Power and Influence* (1953). He neither possessed nor required executive authority or power. But because he was able, so convincingly, to argue the consequences for government of *not* doing what he proposed, he achieved most of what he set out to do.

WHEN NOT TO COMMUNICATE

Leakage of information is due either to lack of loyalty or to lack of discretion among those to whom you communicate the plot.

Machiavelli

Influence relationships, just like business deals, frequently collapse because information about them leaks out. So when you are communicating with whomsoever you want to influence, do not communicate the fact to the wider world. Influence derives much if not most of its strength from being secret. Opponents will try to diminish the relationship by shining a public searchlight on it if they can, just as, for example, political parties will expose the source of the opposition's party funds to destroy or discredit that particular influence.

So beware of yelling too loudly about what you are intending or of giving any indication, either to the person being influenced or to your opponents, what your objectives are. But while the key to a good manipulative relationship is to ensure that Mr B is not altogether aware what effect Mr A will have on him, some discreet signalling of intentions is still useful. Gentle hints, cool suggestions and low-key messages about the advisability of action X as opposed to action Y are usually more effective as an opening gambit than banging all the arguments down on the table from the outset.

Rule 17

It is seldom profitable to broadcast what you are doing in the influence game.

Rule 18

Persuade the decision-takers that the decision you want is their idea.

This was the signal method of Lord Burghley, Elizabeth I's Treasurer and Secretary of State. Single-handedly he guided her with skill and loyalty throughout her reign, but always with discretion. Cultivating her from an impressionable childhood, he, more than any other, had her ear. For long the most important man in England, he never used his influence directly; rather he worked through the Queen, presenting his decisions as hers. A wave, a nod, a gesture, and those around him knew exactly where they stood.

This is a very useful approach. I have heard Foreign Office advisers saying to their political master things like: 'Your thinking on the SALT talks, Secretary of State, is as follows . . .' and Alexander Haig insisting, 'You should remember, Mr President, that your stance on Latin American debts is . . .'. In other words, 'I, the humble adviser, am merely reminding you of your own views, decisions, policies or whatever.' Obsequious maybe, but it works.

A final point on communicating. No matter how influential you are, unless you are in close proximity to your decision-taker you will lose out. An adviser in a private office in London, if that is where the action is, will win hands down over a more able one in New York. Unless the decision-taker is an up-to-the-minute man in terms of electronic communications, the face-to-face situation tends to triumph.

This is one aspect of the exciting and very precise matter of any adviser's position in the office.

Rule 19

If you are next door to the target decision-taker's inner sanctum you will always stand a better chance than more senior people down the corridor.

This I call 'private officemanship', a phenomenon particularly noticeable in the latter part of 1986 and in 1987 with the power struggle that went on over who ruled in the White House in terms of controlling access to President Reagan. Chiefs-of-staff came and went. In the end Nancy ruled the roost.

An excellent example of how immediate accessibility works is demonstrated by the fact that among the British Prime Minister's private secretaries (whatever party is in office) there is always one appointed from the Foreign Office. The person in this slot often has more influence than the rest of the department put together. If he is against some aspect of Foreign Office briefing, then it is within his effective competence to make sure it is ignored. Loyalty to his department of origin is often strained by the more immediate demands of loyalty to the PM and his views. Some become very unpopular with the Foreign Office but cannot be removed or replaced because they have become so indispensable at No 10 Downing Street.

The 'position in office' rule is not absolute. Now, with video phones and Fax machines, comes:

> ### Rule 20
>
> **The importance of geographical proximity varies in inverse proportion to the facility of communications between the parties concerned.**

Part Three
Devious Devices

Chapter 10
Facts

Men ever praise the olden time, and find fault with the present, though often without reason.... Having grown old, they also laud all they remember to have seen in their youth. Their opinion is generally erroneous.... We never know the whole truth about the past.

Machiavelli

It may seem strange to you to begin a section on devious devices with a chapter called 'Facts'. If so, go to the bottom of the class. Facts are the most devious of devices in the whole armoury of the influence game. And, as my economics professor, Tom Johnston, used to say, statistics are worse.

Facts influence. A salient fact is that facts are revered by people who cannot contradict them. Mark Twain pointed out that we all know for certain many facts that are not true, and the political journalist and commentator Brian Walden goes on from there to suggest that little of what we think we know about the famous is true. He adds that, unless there is overwhelming evidence for it, 'Reported speech – quotation marks – are the biggest liars of all.' How true in the pursuit of influence. Did X really advocate Y? Where is the proof, you should ask, unless of course you are using such quotes for your own ends.

Like statistics, facts are extremely dangerous if they get into the wrong hands. They must be controlled and revealed only where essential. The manipulation of information, whether official or unofficial, is one of the most significant of all the tools of influence. When it is mishandled, as by the British government during the *Spycatcher* affair, it can have disastrous results. Facts are the real reason why open government will never work. The more explicitly available the information, the less flexible does the decision-making process become.

Whatever the provenance, items of information or disinformation, particularly when they get into newspaper clipping libraries, become facts for ever. Therefore use the following with especial care: reports, memoranda, statistical analyses, computer printouts, inventories, profit charts and love letters. Like Mark Twain, remember that 'Facts, or what a man believes to be facts, are delightful. ... Get your facts first, and then you can distort them as much as you please.'

Always search for and present unsettling facts. They are usually there if you want them. But be careful. In a by-election an unsavoury fact produced about an opponent at the right time *can* swing things your way, but at the wrong time it can backfire if you are accused of mudslinging. This was exemplified during the 1987 general election campaign when 'revelations' about Tories Jeffrey Archer and Cecil Parkinson, the Liberal leader David Steel and the Labour deputy leader Roy Hattersley seemed actually to help those maligned.

Facts lie behind the modern phenomenon of, in Britain, royal commissions and, in the United States, Senate investigations. This has reached a very fine art in the United Kingdom. Once a royal commission (or a commission of enquiry or other such) has been appointed studying of the facts of a case can serve to postpone a decision for years.

Rule 21

By all means tell the truth but seldom reveal the whole truth.

Chapter 11
Causes and Conflicts

Consolidate the attention of the people against a single adversary – taking care that nothing will split up this attention ... and make different opponents appear as if they belonged to one category.

Adolf Hitler

Hitler's exhortation is dangerous but frequently successful. One of the best devices to marshal people behind you when you want them to follow a given course of action is to create a cause, even if that cause does not actually exist. This is the 'united we stand, divided we don't get anywhere' argument. Pull out all the full-stop words you can muster.

A small, indeed a tiny group within a great company or organization can have a disproportional influence on the whole. Influence is exercised through the perceived exclusivity of the small group (or caucus), which it creates by controlling access to itself and by keeping other pressure groups and potential influents at bay, away from the target decision-taker. One way of doing this is by creating and stimulating shared convictions between the group and the target, defining, for example, the guiding creed or ethic of the whole organization on the lines of – 'In this company only Rule X works'. Such is the position of Ralph (now Lord) Harris and his Institute of Economic Affairs, which has provided the intellectual seedbed for Thatcherism.

In the same way, in the British Foreign Office, Arabists ruled for several decades from the fifties on (until they went out of fashion). Generations of them had attended the same 'public school' – MECAS, the Middle East Centre for Arabic Studies, which, financed by the FO, operated in pre-war-torn Lebanon. The graduates of MECAS (would-be siblings of Lawrence of Arabia, Glubb Pasha and their ilk) shared a love–hate relationship with the Arab world and when they moved on to embassies and missions in other countries, particularly in Paris, Washington and the UN, they dominated much more than the Middle Eastern policies of Britain for a generation. As the desk officer responsible for monitoring the Arab–Israel dispute, I, with no Arabist training, felt their influence enormously. In the most charming, diplomatic way, I was accused of being pro-Israeli, when all I was doing was trying to see the British, rather than the Arab, interests in that enduring conflict. The Foreign Office Arabists had a particularly hard time working with George Brown when he was Foreign Secretary. He had a Jewish wife and knew both sides of the equation better than most. The Arabists – many brilliant men among them – still control some of the best posts in the British Diplomatic Service, but, with the developments of more recent years in the Arab world, they have had to moderate their views.

Every society has its heroes – usually those who, like Robin Hood, Mother Teresa, Danielo Dolci and Vincent de Paul, have campaigned in support of one of the full-stop concepts mentioned earlier – poverty, hunger, social justice. In lesser ways, others, like the group of American mothers who founded MADD, the campaign against drunken driving, or, in Britain, the often maligned and ridiculed Mary Whitehouse, Victoria Gillick and David Bellamy, crusade for the moral or social values they believe in.

Causes often succeed if well organized, if there is money around and if the top patron or front person has charisma. The Duke of Edinburgh's ceaseless campaign to save some of the world's endangered animal species is an example of a hugely successful cause creation and a means of stirring and influencing governments and peoples around the globe.

However, some sob stories do not work, basically because there is too much sobbing and not enough action devoted to remedying them.

There was no sobbing on the part of Ralph Nader, although in creating his cause, he certainly stirred up many very basic emotions among various sections of the community. A lawyer and consumer advocate, Nader became a folk hero in the 1960s as a champion of the rights of the individual against the power of the big American corporations. He took on the Detroit automobile industry on the issue of car safety, and won. Broadening his fight on behalf of the 'public interest' (a full-stop phrase), he attacked other abuses of state and corporate power. In the late 1960s and early 1970s his consumer rights movement developed into what was sometimes called the fifth estate, an activist group designed to challenge the 'might of the corporate lobbies'. While Naderism in Reagan's America is now associated with the over-regulation of industry, perhaps no other American has been more responsible for concrete improvements in the society we all inhabit.

Nader's influence is a good case study since it depended on three factors:

1 His integrity: he was never apparently interested in personal gain.
2 His skilful use of the media: politicians always feared the adverse publicity he might stir up.
3 His determination not just to expose abuses ('muckraker' though he was called), but always to move on to new, broader issues.

The basic rule for you as an individual is to identify a problem which affects a number of people – say, the need for a pedestrian crossing on a busy road – and then to invite others to share in the problem-solving process. This creates a mutual bond. You may choose other emotive concepts, like 'motherhood' or 'liberty' or 'justice', and weld them into your 'pedestrian crossing now' cause, making the several one. Thus any attack on your little campaign will be an attack on a number of other basic values.

Arouse fear in your audience (an individual, a group or indeed a nation) by emphasizing anticipated threats and dangers (thousands of innocents being mown down by juggernauts), and then reassure them that, if they (a) follow your advice and demonstrate, (b) vote for you or (c) vote against the other chap – the 'do-nothing' or 'it costs too much' brigade – all will be well. If you can make a common cause over pedestrian crossings and the big full-stop issues, you can certainly cope with more day-to-day matters, like keeping someone off the board of directors.

THE LOYALTY FACTOR

> We must indeed all hang together, or most assuredly, we shall all hang separately.
>
> *Benjamin Franklin*

The loyalty factor, one based on family links, a web of friendship or other mutual bonds if you can find them, is invaluable in creating a common cause. The method is to influence or persuade for the old school's/team's sake; for the good of the regiment; for some other class, status, peer or tribal group loyalty; because otherwise the commercial credibility of the company will suffer; for patriotism.

Loyalty to a common cause is particularly required within political parties, as the slightest chinks in unity will quickly be picked up and exploited by opponents. The Willie Whitelaws who appeal for harmony and reassure in the name of unity are much more valuable to the Tory Party than the Norman Tebbits and Michael Heseltines, for all their angular activity. Political parties may need thinkers and doers; they also need moderators, to conciliate, to call for loyalty to the common weal in the spirit of whatever it is that is considered important (e.g. unity rather than policy), and to ask for obedience to the leadership of the day.

PULL-THROUGH: THE HOOK AND LINE APPROACH

'Pull-through' is a Harvard Business School term to describe the ploy of using one good cause or concept (i.e. something that will appeal to your target decision-taker) to pull lesser common-cause ideas (or less attractive ones) along. Thus 'We must show the world that we will not be bullied' is followed by 'We must therefore send warships to the Gulf'; 'We must cut back drastically on our overheads' is followed by 'We must sack Jones.'

Basically this is what common causing is all about. If it fails, move on to look for a conflict that unites.

CREATING A CONFLICT

> Smart sayings, when they border on the truth, leave a bitter taste behind them.
>
> *Machiavelli*

This is the reverse of common causing and means finding an issue that will divide your opponents. We have all worked in situations in which everybody gangs up on one person who is blocking some particular policy. Taking this a step further, you can influence through finding and developing sometimes quite small differences between potential rivals – differences of personality, policy, approach or creed – which can then be inflated. You yourself should remain aloof from the conflict until the right moment. Fend off both sides if they try to enlist your support. Appear as honest broker. Let them weaken and destroy each other, then walk in, like Fortinbras in the final scene of *Hamlet*, and pick up the pieces and the glory.

Conflicts within an office can be a useful way of getting to core objectives, as President Kennedy found. On the other side of the coin, his successor, Jimmy Carter, was at the centre of competing groups which led to a diplomatic shambles. At the heart of the problem was the personality and policy friction between the then Secretary of State, Cyrus Vance, and the National Security Adviser, Zbigniew Brzezinski, over how to deal with the Soviet Union: wield the big stick or go for a more conciliatory approach. The name of the game, to quote the former British Ambassador, Sir Nicholas Henderson, was not so much who was right but who was getting credit for what.

Trade union leaders in Britain have long been thought of and accused of creating conflicts for their own ends. A strong union leader has to lead and, almost by definition, he will seek to be more militant than the majority of the members. Someone who leads from behind will soon be pushed out. In contrast, Norman Willis, the present Secretary-General of the TUC, has a reputation as mediator and his strength lies in his abilities as a conciliator. Much can be achieved by someone good at building bridges. Removing conflict, usually a much more difficult task than creating it, can buy much influence too, provided it is seen as a strength and not a weakness.

In an earlier age Prince Metternich, the Austrian diplomat, played a divisive hand with consummate skill. He manipulated Austria's great neighbours, Russia and France, and, with that other great wielder of influence of the time, Talleyrand, played a dominant role in redrawing the map of Europe after the defeat of Napoleon. His major weakness lay in a complacent self-certainty and the fact that his channels of information were not always as effective as they should have been. He was aware of the forces of nationalism that swept through Austria in 1848, but when they hit he was unprepared.

He is not alone in the history of those in high office who, cocooned in Downing Street, the White House or presidential palaces around the globe, have lost touch with reality. It takes a strong person to perceive reality and not reflection when it is distorted by the mirrors of television and the press. In such circumstances the divide and rule technique can be and often is brought into play. For politics within organizations, as everyone knows, can be more fun, more exhausting, more time-consuming than the real thing. This was particularly true during Harold Wilson's prime-ministership. He may not have chosen to create a conflict among his advisers, but it happened none the less, and policy making, as subsequent memoirs have made abundantly clear, tended to take second place to whether his press secretary, Joe Haines, or his political adviser, Marcia Williams, won the day.

A telling sign of weakness in any organization is, consequently, when the middle men are at daggers drawn. Warring robber barons use up all their energy in fighting each other rather than in working for the common weal. Watch out for this and do not get drawn in; instead, use it to your advantage. If you want to get rid of the quarrelling, do what leaders from the Romans to Reagan and a multitude of other politicians and businessmen have done – find an external enemy to deflect attention from internal problems and to unite against. If that fails, then either sack the miscreants, move them to some distant function or promote them to non-executive positions on the board, to the House of Lords, and so on. Machiavelli was thinking on these lines when he advised: 'War should be the only study of a prince. He should consider peace only as a breathing-time, which gives him leisure to contrive, and furnishes ability to execute.'

Both causes and conflicts can always be stirred up with choice yet modest phrases such as:

- 'Far be it from me to take a stand in this controversy, but ...'
- 'It's none of my business, however, ...'
- 'I really don't have a view on this disagreement, though I must say ...'
- 'I'm no expert, but ...'
- 'Can I be quite honest with you, Chairman, ...'
- 'While I share your very desirable objectives/your concerns, I have to say ...'
- 'With respect, sir [even though respect is far from due], ...'
- 'If I may say so ...' (Lord Goodman's favourite)
- 'I agree with you, Minister, you know that. However, the PM and the rest of the Cabinet ...'

But watch out your ploys do not misfire. You can make serious enemies who will go for your weak points. There is no point in yelling like Tarzan and thumping your hairy chest if you are propounding a lost cause.

Chapter 12
Options

Dr Robert Runcie, the Archbishop of Canterbury, has in the past been accused of nailing his colours firmly to the fence. I am not against that as a strategy from time to time, but, in general, living and achieving is all about facing up to the options that daily confront you. It is also about presenting them to others. You have your option that you want to win. The aim is to pass it on to your decision-taker at the best possible moment. Get him to believe, or to come to believe, that the idea is in his best interests – indeed, that it is his idea – with choice phrases, such as 'I've always respected your belief, Chairman, that maximizing sales comes first ...' or 'Given your deep understanding of the market for soapsuds, I can see why you feel that ...'. You can also use this device when trying to persuade, not just your decision-taker, but a wider public.

Create the right environment, as, for example, the Anti-Smoking and Health (ASH) group has done by making smoking socially unacceptable, or like campaigns that have projected drinking and driving as a social stigma, and you will have a better chance of success.

Another useful stratagem is to transfer responsibility for advocating a particular option to someone whom the target decision-taker respects: 'The Chairman is coming down in favour of ...', 'I know the Prime Minister feels ...', 'The Director-General has it in mind ...'. or try throwing him a challenge: 'I know only you can do it/bring it off.' Just as he is making up his mind, clinch the matter with: 'A brilliant idea of yours, if I may say so.'

Do not push too hard; trying to coerce always brings repercussions. Arguments, even if you win them, are never for the best.

Let the other person do most of the talking. Keep seeing, and saying you are seeing, things from his point of view.

There are a number of phrases which are useful in getting colleagues to adopt your particular option, particularly if you can create allies by offering praise in the process. Thus: 'The Finance Director is very experienced in this area and I fully agree with him. However, I'd like to take it a step further and ...'; or 'I'm so glad George mentioned that. It reinforces my view that ...'; or 'The Chairman has asked a very pertinent question. The answer is, of course, clear ...'; or 'Absolutely right. But let me put it another way ...' (which is totally different, of course). Weasel words do butter parsnips.

THE THREE-OPTIONS APPROACH

Everyone reacts in different ways to different situations, but if you can control some of the choices open to the decision-taker you end up points ahead. To this end, the Three-Options Approach is a very handy little device. Present your decision-taker (minister, managing director, head of department) with three options, each carefully set out and given apparently equal weight, but make sure that two of them fall short of what is really required (do not make them too patently absurd). The third option – the one you want – goes through. This is a classic way of ensuring that a preferred candidate for a job will be selected. If the other runners are well below par, yours will be chosen.

> Rule 22
>
> **Present a range of options, but have one ready that stands out.**

As a cautionary note, however, it is worth remembering the story about a Treasury interview at which the mandarins put up a nonentity to make sure that their preferred man would get the job.

The nonentity rose to the occasion and performed so well that he got the appointment. No plan is ever totally foolproof.

A similar case occurred while I was in the Foreign Office. The Prime Minister, who had final say on senior ambassadorial appointments, was offered two pathetic and one outstanding candidate for a prestigious embassy job. One of the incompetents was selected.

History is littered with like examples. It is not unknown for a Director-General of the BBC to be chosen because the board of governors was unable to decide as between two front-runners.

Never present just two options, one obviously good and the other poor. Any decision-taker worth his salt will simply start identifying third, fourth and fifth options to pursue.

OTHER PEOPLE'S OPTIONS

Rule 23

Create the feeling that the opposition is inadequate, seldom that it is dangerous.

Avoid knocking other people's options too openly. It is much better gradually to ensure that everyone thinks all the other man's ideas are unworkable. Suggest widespread disillusionment. Have a few choice retorts discreetly at the ready, if possible rubbishing both the idea and the man at the same time. As La Rochefoucauld advised, 'Wit sometimes enables us to act rudely with impunity,' so make your remarks amusing, even if unfair. A feeling of inadequacy about the opposition can often be created by simple scorn. Good examples include:

- 'Goodness gracious. He's not come up with that old one again.'
- 'Well, you have to give him something for persistence.'
- 'It's better than his last idea for developing gold out of seaweed-/marketing English sliced bread in France, etc.'

- 'He would say that, wouldn't he?'
- 'That's what that Trotskyite/fascist/woolly Liberal, etc., would argue.'
- 'That's the ticket if you're talking in terms of narrow self-interest.'
- 'Oh, they've let him out again, have they?'
- 'He tried it on the Opposition when they were in power. They actually *liked* it.'
- 'Poor old George. Time to go out to grass, don't you think?'

A final thought on proffering options. If your decision-taker has Machiavelli as his bedtime reading, he may remember the following passage:

> A prince must always seek advice. But he must do so when he wants to, not when others want him to; indeed, he must discourage everyone from tendering advice unless it is asked. All the same, he should be a constant questioner and he should listen patiently to the truth regarding what he has inquired about. ... So the conclusion is that good advice, whomever it comes from, depends on the shrewdness of the prince who seeks it.

Chapter 13
Moral and Immoral Mechanisms

CREEPING INFLUENCE

> Tender your advice with modesty.
>
> *Machiavelli*

Oozing under doors and through cracks can sometimes get you where you want to go faster than full-frontal exposure. Good middlemen, company secretaries and senior civil servants recognize the truth of this assertion. But because the incremental method takes time, if you intend to operate in this way, do not lose sight of long-term objectives. And do not be seen to be wasting time – theirs or yours. In other words, the influential person often achieves more by walking slowly than by running fast.

Move from one minor decision to the next, never threatening revolution with big issues. Present one decision at a time, each one hardly a problem.

HYPE

> It is the hinge that squeaks that gets the grease.
>
> *Malcolm X*

One of the greatest of all dubious devices – along with 'facts' – is hype. Hype goes far beyond mere facts. Indeed, it is worth a book in itself. It is a form of attempted mega-influence or persuasion. Behind-the-scenes hype can often be effective and is always far from worthless. Up-front hype, particularly if megawords about megadom are used, is so common and debased that even the hoi polloi ignore it.

The most recently discovered pop star, the latest film, the newest blockbuster, the up-to-the-minute diet, the current life-style fad is Fantastic, Devastating, Sensational, Unique, Exclusive, Incredible, No. 1, Super-duper, Percipient, Best-selling, Oscar-worthy (not just for films), and so on. Hype, which overemphasizes the key points, is fed to the mass media and thus to the masses by individuals and public relations men and women, who try to make the recipients believe that what they are being told is unadulterated, objective fact, when all it is is hype.

Too often hype convinces the object of the hype as well. A lot of nonsense is said about the importance and influence of certain individuals. Beware the man who has become legend in his own mind, who goes around punching the world with his own import-ance and dynamism.

On the positive side, Bob Geldof's enormously successful campaign for Band Aid was a form of hype – for the best of causes. Geldof himself, known initially only to the youthful followers of pop culture, rocketed to greater things through his enormous personal energy and drive. His influence, once perceived, grew ever greater. He was and is the great arm-twister, the supreme lobbyist. Without doubt, the millions of pounds collected for Africa would not have been raised without him. He saw the problem and the solution and, by hyping them, made others see them too.

Good hype can be immensely powerful. The only thing wrong with hype is some of the noise it makes. Bad hype is bad only because the end is bad, not because of the techniques used. In a way it is merely the inverse of restrained authority, the perceived power factor working hyper-successfully.

One version of hype is used daily, particularly in the news media. They hype both themselves and their stories with buzzwords such as 'exclusive', 'scoop' and so on. But there are other words and phrases which are used much more cleverly, to persuade and influence.

EMOTIVE WORDS AND PHRASES

First Salesman: I made some excellent contacts today.
Second Salesman: I didn't get any orders either.

Leader writers, particularly in the heavy Sunday papers, love certain words and phrases. Recently I found the following (excluding full-stop words) in a *Sunday Telegraph* editorial:

- *relevant*, as in 'That is a very relevant argument' and 'The TV programme was highly relevant to today's problems.'
- *valid*, as in 'His argument is valid in every sense of the word' (how many senses of the word 'valid' are there?)
- *influential* – 'Influential politicians argue ...' (whom do they influence?)
- *unquestionably* – 'It is unquestionably the case that ...' (apartheid is wrong, as it happens) 'but ...' (the writer went on)
- *arguably* (this was used three times), as in 'This is arguably the best way to proceed' (well, is it or isn't it?)

Certain adjectives are also frequently employed to impress, though they usually obscure. They include: optimum, ongoing, integral, conceptual, functional, reciprocal, multilateral and global. If other people use them, react sharply.

Note all such words well. Do not despise them. Most people do not question them, so they can be used to add weight to an argument.

PLAYING ON STRESS

A great deal has been written about stress in recent times. We all know about it. We all sometimes recognize it in ourselves. How can we use it?

Few senior people in the business world take stress seriously since, according to a director of the Stress Research and Management Unit at St Bartholomew's Hospital, they simply pass their stress-inducing problems down the line. As a result it is the middle managers who suffer stress.

We have all read about what causes stress: change of job, divorce, moving house and so on bring on anything from high blood pressure to alcoholism. The would-be influent therefore must not ignore stress either in him/herself or in others.

People react to stress in two totally opposite ways: fight or flight. Make sure you know your man before you try the stress game. Putting him under pressure may merely lead to his adrenaline flowing faster and his winning hands down. That said, it sometimes helps to point out any pressures that will help to force along your proposed course of action. Included among these are:

- pressure of time: a major decision has to be taken in the next 3 minutes. (Lack of time concentrates the mind like nothing else.)
- pressure of money: interest rates go up at midnight. Every moment of delay counts.
- pressure of competition: the opposition are on their way here with a better offer.
- social pressures: what will your mother-in-law (etc.) think when I tell her?

Rule 24

Intelligent Perception of options decreases as stress increases.

Stress factors have to be employed with care: they can be counter-productive if you force them too hard. Your successful decision-taker may have been learning how to cope with stress for much longer than you have. Creating stress in others can be equally telling on you. You may be the one to burn out in the end. A senior public relations consultant of my acquaintance thought he was winning hands down in getting a major customer away from one of his rivals. His opponent's marriage was cracking up and he played on this fact, waiting for his victim's business acumen to crumble. What happened was that his rival's wife's departure was just what his rival needed to remove stress. My PR man lost his deal.

RIDICULE

> Ridicule is more deadly than all the arguments in the world.
>
> *Frederick the Great*

One of the most formidable ways of increasing stress in a person is to make him feel a fool, laughed at, mocked. Even the strongest find this difficult to bear. Ridicule is the 'like being savaged by a dead sheep' line, as Denis Healey said of British Foreign Secretary Geoffrey Howe.

Again, people react in different ways. Sir Clive Sinclair hated the mockery that greeted his electric car. Sir Ralph Halpern appeared to ride the storm of his sexual adventure with some ease.

Ridicule is a dangerous tool. It is possible to destroy someone utterly, not so much by making him look a fool at a particular time, but by ensuring the permanence of the ridicule. A few words will often suffice, particularly if you hit the right note, as F. R. Leavis did when he dismissed the Sitwells for belonging to the world of publicity, not of art.

Particularly effective is the nudge, nudge, wink, wink, approach: every time a person's name is mentioned a snigger goes round the room because the name is automatically linked to some defect (for example, 'Gerald Ford, the man who can't walk and chew gum at the same time.')

Choose something that sticks, either a nickname – e.g. 'the Loony Left' – or a pejorative prefix – e.g. 'poor old ...' – used every time the person's name is mentioned. Other examples are: 'I'd like a second opinion on the Leader of the Opposition – from a taxidermist' (said by David Lange, Prime Minister of New Zealand); 'He has completed the long road to the lunatic asylum of politics' (Richard Cottrell, MEP, on Tony Benn); 'Far better [for him] to keep his mouth shut and let everyone think he's stupid than to open it and leave no doubt' (Norman Tebbit on Dennis Skinner).

The British satirical magazine *Private Eye* uses ridicule to some effect, choosing schoolboy nicknames (the Abominable Goodman, Goodmanzee, Victor 'disgusting' Lowndes, Pirana Teeth Stevens, etc.) for public figures who gradually come to bear a striking resemblance to their sobriquets.

Ridicule through art and literature is as old as time. Modern cartoonists such as Trog or Scarfe are working in the shade of Hogarth and Gillray. A devastating cartoon can be a powerful weapon, as can the puppetry of 'Spitting Image', which reputedly damaged David Steel's election prospects. Similarly, the television programme 'That Was the Week that Was', successfully ridiculed a whole generation of public figures.

Rule 25

Beware the dangers of wit and humour. Decision-takers may not appreciate mockery; opponents may actually benefit from being mocked.

Remember, as Thomas Jefferson said, 'Resort is had to ridicule only when reason is against us.'

MAKE THEM LAUGH

... in your report here, it says that you are an extremely dull person. Our experts describe you as an appallingly dull fellow, unimaginative, timid, spineless, easily dominated, no sense of humour, tedious company and irrepressibly drab and awful. And whereas in most professions these would be considered drawbacks, in accountancy they are a positive boon.

John Cleese et al.

Telling a joke can make people like you or hate you. It can also help persuade. Humour, if properly used, can implant ideas in people's minds well beyond the humour itself, as John Cleese has so successfully demonstrated in his training films (the joke about accountants is not taken from one of them) and television advertisements. He believes that getting people to laugh at themselves and others, particularly over their received opinions and prejudices, helps them change for the better and look at problems in a new light. And laughter helps make ideas and concepts stick.

SEXUAL INFLUENCE

Losing my virginity was a career move.

Madonna

History is littered with the devastated careers of those who have fallen (and, *pace* Madonna, risen) as a result of sexual influence. Mata Haris exist in every walk of life. Sex or the denial of it is, provenly, one of the key influences in modern business, political and social life. It exists, man over woman, woman over man, man over man, woman over woman, and leads to gossip, blackmail, scandal, divorce, violence and every banner headline in the tabloid editor's book.

Rule 26

Watch sex. It is the key to success and the trap door to failure.

Messalina, the child wife of the Roman emperor Claudius, was notorious for her avarice, lust and cruelty. She could incite her meek and doting husband to hideous acts by a combination of a devious mind and sensuously beautiful body. She could and did get away with murder, Claudius recognizing no defect in her, until her public 'marriage' (in his absence) to one of her many lovers led even him to realize her worth. He promptly made up for lost time and had her executed.

While caution and the libel laws forbid too many contemporary examples, the British political and commercial scene has always been titillatingly littered with sexual scandal, usually arising when influence has gone wrong or when the central character has refused to allow himself to be blackmailed. This tends to lead to revelation. Sometimes the victims, like the War Minister, John Profumo, who shared a mistress with a Soviet military attaché, or, latterly, Cecil Parkinson, the chairman of the Conservative Party, have to go. However, like Mr Parkinson and doubtless eventually Jeffrey Archer, some fall only to rise again.

At the time of the 1987 British general election a spate of top names appeared in the tabloid press. In all cases there appeared to be no clear agent of influence who might reap anything other than destructive benefits from the situation. Or was there? There was indeed. What motive did the popular press have in pursuing these cases? It was not out of any high-minded desire to uphold moral standards (whatever the leader writers might claim in their editorials) but, quite simply, an attempt to increase their own circulation figures. Given that the British public tends to buy the worst media product at the expense of the best, the tabloids always win handsomely by revealing the sexual indiscretions of the great of the land. Pop stars are another target. The *Sun* actually boasted of its circulation triumphs as a result of publishing so-called revelations about the singer Elton John.

In the matter of public hypocrisy in its attitude towards sexual influence gone wrong, America is now not far behind Britain. Again, the media exploit both for their own benefit as well as to bring (for reasons of spite?) the powerful to their knees. The American press was the last to lose in its inquiries that led Miss Donna Rice, speaking of Gary Hart, to claim that 'Sex was not part of our relationship'. Few believed her, any more than that the powerful Congressman

Wilbur Mills could survive after revelations of an affair with a torrid stripper, the aptly named Fanne Fox. These things come in waves, all the more so at periods when public morality is an issue. And how much more popular is the victim's downfall if, like the evangelist, Jim Bakker, who dallied with one Jessica Hahn, that victim is an erstwhile leader of the so-called moral majority.

The rich and famous (usually men) of all generations – Warren Harding, Franklin Roosevelt, Lloyd George, John F. Kennedy – apparently lapsed with much younger women. By and large they got away with it. Quite often, however, it is the smaller fry that fall from grace, often as a result of precise entrapment. Hence the fortunes of the marines guarding the US Embassy in Moscow, who in return for sexual favours gave the KGB a guided tour of (and an apparent opportunity to plant microphones in) the most secret of diplomatic places. The Russians have always been good at the beautiful-spy technique: it is now well known that Sir Geoffrey Harrison, the British Ambassador to Moscow in the 1960s, had to resign over a brief dalliance with a Russian chambermaid at his official residence.

I have concentrated on the influence of women over men since, historically and with a few well-known exceptions, most societies have tended to make the man the decision-taker. In the modern Western world things have changed rapidly, however, and there are now many women in positions of great authority. In working to get there they have a particularly difficult and dangerous time. The sexual politics of any organization, from the Cabinet room (certain ministers have made extremely sexist remarks about the femininity of Mrs Thatcher) to the boardroom, is always doomladen. If they are very attractive and well turned out, women have to work especially hard (a) to be taken seriously; (b) *not* to be regarded merely as the statutory female or worse; (c) to avoid being typified as a dilettante or dumb blonde who is 'only playing at it'; (d) to avoid being accused of being too emotional; (e) to escape the put down that 'she'll crack as soon as her child gets the mumps' or 'it must be the time of the month' or 'she'd never be ruthless enough'.

As one of my current colleagues suggests, 'If a woman achieves a position of real influence *and* retains her femininity, then men feel threatened by the knowledge that she has had to be twice as talented and competent as her male counterpart to achieve the same status.'

We may or may not agree with Macaulay when he said, 'We know of no spectacle so ridiculous as the British public in one of its periodic fits of morality.' It does not matter. The threat of exposure over some straight or crooked sexual activity usually has a fairly definite effect. I have mentioned some of the stories that broke. By the very nature of this most secretive area of influence – which merges effortlessly into blackmail – how many more cases are there in which pressure/influence/blackmail was successful simply because it was undetected?

We do not need to worry too much about the ethics of the media revealing details about public figures' private lives. Politicians, whatever they may say, are only too happy to reveal details about their private lives when it suits them – their generosity, their happy family life, their churchgoing and so on. They are thus on shaky ground when they try to define which private parts are private. After all, the good bits and the bad both affect how people vote.

BACKSCRATCHING FOR BEGINNERS

We are now at the sharp end of the influence game: the purchase of what is wanted – the bait, financial or other, followed by the calling in of favours given.

It is very easy, even for intelligent people, to fall into the trap of being devious. This easily leads to mild corruption. Then comes gentle bribery, blackmail, lying and cheating. Quite apart from the moral issues, being found out means that you slide rapidly to the right along the influence spectrum until you have zero effect. The City of London and Wall Street are littered with the corpses of analysts, businessmen and financiers who got too clever, among them Boesky, Saunders and Collier.

When someone says that he isn't in something for the money but as a matter of principle, it is usually the money he is after. Some people easily and subtly anaesthetize themselves, as, step by step, innocent favours become something more. Eventually they scarcely notice when they adopt any of the following:

- the 'you do this for me and I'll do this for you' option;
- the gentle art of the unspoken bribe – the freebie, the junket, the 'favour';
- the explicit promotion of the 'common interest' factor.

Then they move effortlessly on to bribery or palm-greasing.

An interesting study can be made of why small favours can win great rewards when very expensively purchased campaigns fail. If this is your preferred method of working, what you may need are access to free tickets to *Cats*, Lord's, Covent Garden or the Cup Final. You're in another league when it comes to crates of gin, beautiful (preferably fallen) women (or men), holidays in the Bahamas, suitcases of unmarked greenbacks, or the wherewithal to provide the odd life peerage or knighthood. If it really is just a favour – pantomime tickets for the children – that is OK. The whole business entertainment industry is perceived to be perfectly respectable. You entertain to the top of your expense account in order to influence. If it is more than that and there is an obvious tat for the tit, the favour is a bribe, particularly if it becomes known. Dangerous stuff.

That is why in Britain and America government ministers and civil servants may not receive a gift above a certain purely token value. If they have to accept valuable presents so as not to cause offence, as HM Ambassadors in the Gulf States did during the Queen's visit to the region, they display them for the brief duration of the visit and then sadly turn them in to the Foreign Office, which sells them off and keeps the money. And that, presumably, is all right.

These, then, are some of the devices which can be used in order to influence and persuade. But they are dull and lifeless tools unless you yourself are personally capable of handling and exploiting them and of being believed. To this end you can actually *learn* certain techniques of self-presentation when you are in meetings, being interviewed or addressing a wider gathering, either around a table or in a large conference hall, and that is the subject matter of the next section.

Part Four
Learnable Skills

Chapter 14
Interview Techniques

Everyone sees what you appear to be; few experience what you really are.

Machiavelli

We have talked in general terms about how to identify and present yourself, your ideas and ambitions in the light of your assessment both of your target and of any opposition you are likely to face. Now we are going to be precise and talk about self-presentation in two very important fields of influence: in interview (be it for the media or for a job, the techniques are surprisingly similar) and, in front of a sizable audience. Having taught the disciplines I have to admit that there is no substitute for learning from a professional instructor, but you can still pick up many of the basic skills from the written word.

Since these skills can be used in other settings, both in business and everyday encounters, I go on to explain the rules of negotiation and how to manage committees. Presentation of self can become a *very* exact study in all four fields.

HOW DO YOU LOOK? HOW DO YOU SOUND?

You may be good, even very good, at putting your case across to close colleagues and familiar clients in normal day-to-day exchanges. But your self-projection may pale when exposed to the bright lights of a television studio or an audience of shareholders. Nervousness and a lack of technique are the principal causes. The result is that you present yourself and your arguments badly, be it in a television interview, at a hostile business meeting or when merely making an after-dinner speech in unfamiliar surroundings. Many an outstanding businessman suffers dreadfully from stage fright.

Rule 27

First impressions count. Second impressions count even more.

You can improve your performance if you learn to control and use the tension to which every speaker is subject and to analyse your own performance – cutting out or using unconscious mannerisms of speech or delivery to your advantage. Needless to say, knowledge of your subject matter is the first step to fuller confidence.

There are two accepted ways of learning if you agree to swallow your pride and cope with some short-lived embarrassment. Both require you to understand how bad you are at the moment. One is to enrol with a professional teacher for training sessions with a small group of your colleagues. Peer group criticism in a studio or a 'laboratory' environment is by far the best teacher. The other is to use video-playback tuition, what might be termed the 'shock' technique. Most companies specializing in this field use cameras to film your efforts and then play back the result to you. If nothing else, this will tell you very quickly if you need elocution lessons.

You will certainly learn from your own mistakes. Common faults include: the irresolute look; nervous hand movements and twitches (if you have a tendency to fiddle, turn your hand movements into gestures and make them in style); the way you sit (unless you can lounge in a posture of effortless superiority, sit four-square and upright – it makes you look as if you mean what you say). These and a host of other faults can easily be remedied, particularly by constant rehearsal.

Just as it takes practice to get rid of irritating mannerisms, so you have to learn to use good ones to advantage. Knowing when to look at the camera and when at the interviewer, and developing some of the skills of the acting profession can take you a very long way.

The British Conservative Party is no longer content to leave such matters up to the whim of the individual and has employed a fashion consultant to advise MPs on how to dress and style themselves – so-called 'power dressing'. The manner in which the party went about this was, admittedly, a splendid exercise in how not to do such things, and the papers were full of quotes from indignant Tory women who felt that they were quite all right as they were, thank you, but that the ladies of the SDP might benefit from similar treatment.

But the idea is a good one, particularly for television interviews. Conventional clothes are best, and avoid extreme colours: grey rather than very dark or light suits for men, pastels for women. White with a dark colour is difficult for the camera and men should make sure that tie and shirt do not clash. Women should avoid wearing too much jewellery, while for men, gold chains, straining shirt buttons, gaps between sock and trouser leg or greasy hair are out.

If you are offered it, a touch of powder make-up is a good idea. Nothing spoils an interview more than a sheen of sweat on the brow and upper lip and any blemishes or spots are accentuated by studio lighting and thus best disguised.

DO'S AND DON'TS IN THE STUDIO

- Choose a stable, upright chair.
- Lean forward a little, square on to the camera if possible. Never slouch, no matter how comfortable the chair.
- Always look at the interviewer or whoever is talking; do not look at the camera.
- Don't allow your eyes to wander to the left or the right or you will appear shifty.

– Pull your jacket well down at the back or else you will look hunched as if you have no neck. Men should sit on the tail of their jacket.

In a radio, television or press interview, remember that you know more about what you want to say than the interviewer does. You must make sure you say it, despite what the interviewer tries to make you say. The tighter you say your piece the better. But a good interviewer will prepare himself, and will often be better briefed than the victim expects (e.g. 'In 1972 you actually said the exact opposite to what you are saying now. I have here your exact words . . .'). Every interviewer has his own technique. Try to get hold of a tape of him at work and study it. Always remember that what he wants out of the interview is radically different from what you want.

There are twelve basic 'bewares' for television interviewees:

1 Beware of being quoted out of context. Remember, your most controversial remark is the one that will win any headline, so choose it with care. Make your most important point in a single sentence. If the interview is quite long, have a persuasive one-sentence conclusion at the ready. Try to have the last word.

2 Beware of being edited down. A reasoned argument can end up as a few seconds of television time or a few lines of copy in a newspaper report, and the editing will always seem unfair. So try to appear live if you can and keep your key answers as short as possible. You will never have as much time as you want in which to say your piece. If you only have two minutes, throw in everything you've got. In that way you will attract people's attention. My own proclivity to labour a point was subdued on one occasion, temporarily at least, by John Cleese, who interrupted one of my more ponderous observations with 'Michael, you are giving a new meaning to the term "chaise longue".'

3 Beware of sounding out of date. News today is not news tomorrow. Timing is all. Try to get what you want out when it suits you. Make sure you know when the interview is going to be screened, otherwise it may appear dated.

4 Beware the human-interest story: it will always win hands down over the hard truth. If you are being interviewed about sacking somone for being idle, corrupt and dishonest, even if he is all those things, but looks a pitiful victim with an old, infirm mother, you will lose your case. In the same way, bad news you don't want publicized always wins out over good news. Don't defend; always attack in such circumstances.

5 Beware of being interviewed 'down the line', that is, from a remote studio with your face appearing on a monitor screen. People always look wooden in such situations, and your appearance will not be helped by the fact that the hearing aid you have to wear looks exactly like a hearing aid. It usually works badly into the bargain.

6 Beware of being sidetracked. The interviewer may become aggressive or change tack. If you want to be successful, you must rise above it. Don't get angry and don't over-react. Sidetrack the interviewer if things get tough.

7 Beware of being caught off guard. Do things in your own time. Use the 'not now, but I'll speak to you on my own ground in an hour's time' technique. Find out who else will be appearing with you. Make sure you know what, if any, back-up film is being screened to attack or illustrate your position.

8 Beware of having words put into your mouth. If the interviewer begins, 'Don't you agree that the present situation ...', warning lights should start to flash. If you reply, 'Yes, well, I suppose. . . ', you are sunk.

9 Beware of the same question being put in different ways. The distinguished psychiatrist, Dr Anthony Clare, knows how to keep asking questions to draw out what he wants to know from a patient, a lunch companion or a public figure in his BBC Radio series 'In the Psychiatrist's Chair'. He doesn't waste time asking pointless questions or putting himself forward unless it is to elicit a response from his interviewee. The kindest question is often the most deadly.

10 Beware statements such as 'We already know from Mr X or Miss Y all about Z.' This is the age-old 'all we are seeking is confirmation' approach. Don't be fazed. Don't be cowed by aggression. Be positive and stick to your guns.

11 Beware the negative question, the 'when did you stop beating your wife' trick. It is as old as time and frequently effective. Watch out for being asked to deny something. The next day the headlines will run: 'Mr X denied last night that he was a drug-crazed, tax-evading pederast.'

12 Beware of alcohol. Never have a drink before an interview. It always shows.

On the positive side, remember the following tips: jargon should be avoided like the plague, and, if you can manage it (and only if you are absolutely sure of yourself), a little humour can win you a lot of brownie points.

Rule 28

Train yourself to appear genuine and sincere.

Finally, train yourself to look sincere. If you can achieve this you can achieve anything. Most intelligent and articulate people are horrified when they first see themselves on television, but there is nothing to be ashamed of in not being able to talk naturally and convincingly in the artificial surroundings of a television studio. It is possible to practise appearing to be sincere by watching yourself on video or on closed-circuit television. Yes, you too can learn the Alastair Burnet smile, the narrowing of the eyes, the glowing authority.

A number of American commentators thought they learned a lot about 'sincerity' from the television coverage of the Iran–Contra hearings. As one criminal lawyer remarked, 'As someone used to trying to distinguish truth from lies, I believe there is no greater lie detector than television. If you've got something to hide, avoid the cameras like the plague.'

Beyond that, the hearings provided a splendid guide to what to do and what not to do on television. Colonel North, with all his medals ablaze, was steady-eyed, romantic, smart and earnest. He won ten times more supporters than he lost through his apparent inner strength and control under stress, unlike Admiral Poindexter, whose defensiveness (and overly unpleasant lawyer) let him down. George Shultz, by contrast, was firm, decisive and indignant – admitting the negative elements early on and then burying them under the good. He came out of the hearing well, as did Regan, who exuded a charm and humour few knew he possessed.

Incidentally, American media surveys show that most members of the public take to or against a character (real or fictional) within the first fifteen seconds of his or her appearing on the box.

GETTING OUT OF A TRICKY CORNER

Nothing becomes a general more than to anticipate the enemy's plans.

Machiavelli

Some interviewers are out to trap you, particularly if you are defending a controversial or weak case. Again, remember, it is what you want to say that matters. So try changing the interview's direction. It often works.

When asked a difficult question, Denis Healey is good at saying, 'Now, I think the question you are trying to ask me is ...'. He usually gets away with it. Another version is: 'The question you *should* be asking is ...'. This implies that the interviewer is a prize twit and doesn't understand what he is on about.

Or try the following:

- 'You're getting away from the real point ...'
- 'The point *I* am trying to make is ...'
- 'I would put it another way ...'
- 'I thought I'd covered that, but I'll say it again ...'
- 'What I think you are trying to get at is ...'
- 'That's not the real issue ...' (again, this implies the interviewer has got it back to front or gone off on the wrong tack)
- 'You may think that that's what we're getting at, but ...'
- 'I'm glad you asked that question ...' (you're not, so don't answer it, but appearing to approve of the question helps)

Another version is: 'That's a very interesting question, but ...' or, quite simply, 'You've got it all wrong.'

Watch out for: 'Now let me make myself entirely clear ...' (Oh yes?) or 'Far be it from me to ...' (which means the reverse). Much of the above will also be very useful to you if you have to make a public speech and answer questions afterwards. So let us move on to that.

Chapter 15
Public Speaking

Ask yourself whether the person to whom you are about to listen is but a brilliant orator, valiant in words but inexperienced ...

Machiavelli

A sea of faces, a huge room. You stand up. Can you make your speech or will you seize up and your mind go blank? Some of the greatest figures in Britain and the United States both hate and are bad at public speaking. Great orators come but seldom into this world yet effective public speakers can be made. Public speaking is a learnable art, best done with the help of a skilled teacher who will show you how to project your voice with variety and confidence. We spend a lot of time at school learning how to write, but we are seldom taught how to speak, more's the pity. We may never be brilliant. We may never lose our underlying nervousness, but we can hide it. We all can learn how to be informative, coherent and interesting.

At the outset you should find out how big your audience is. As a rule of thumb, the bigger it is, the simpler your message should be. Also, what are the acoustics like? How big is the room? Does it have a loudspeaker system and, if so, does it work properly (half the time it does not). Is there a lectern? If having one gives you added confidence, make sure it is provided. Everyone will see if your hands tend to shake and it will be more obvious if you are holding papers. If there is no lectern, use stiff cards for your notes. Is there enough light for you to see by? Also ask for a glass of water to be provided. Even professionals find their mouth goes dry.

If you are unable to speak in public, whether to a huge auditorium or to an audience of one, you will fail to project yourself and your ideas properly. An ability to give a good presentation can make or break a sale of brushes at the door or a major defence policy change at the Cabinet table. You will be pleasantly surprised at how easily the necessary skills can be mastered – overcoming shyness and nervousness, projecting your voice, presenting the image and the information you want to put across, whether it be impromptu remarks to a group of colleagues or addressing thousands at a national conference. When training people I have found that, for example, simply getting them to speak *much* more loudly than they normally do (even making them shout at me at the beginning of the training session) helps to quell a large part of their anxiety.

There is no excuse for delivering a boring or cliché-ridden speech. Keep it short, uncomplicated and to the point, and if you are not naturally witty, add one good joke, provided you are sure you can deliver it without fluffing the punchline. Know your subject, for unless you do you will be unconvincing. Knowledge is the mother of sincerity.

Rule 29

Keep it brief. You will always be forgiven for a short speech; never for a long one.

It is essential to prepare yourself well. Write for speaking rather than for reading by recording and listening to yourself in advance. Then throw away your text and speak from notes.

The crucial rule is brevity. There is an old saying that an after-dinner speech should be like a lady's dress: long enough to cover the subject and short enough to be interesting.

Keep it simple. What you say should be able to be summed up in one sentence. And keeping it simple always increases the size of your actual audience, for, unless you are a brilliant speaker or have fascinating (to the audience rather than to you) information to impart, you will lose your audience after ten to fifteen minutes. Research shows the average concentration limit is twelve minutes. Over twenty minutes, and even with the help of visual aids, a speech becomes a lecture and your listeners' attention wavers. Make your most important points early and be alert to the boredom/attention threshold.

If you are using audio-visual material, it should be slick, quick and work. Tell your audience how long you are going to speak for and do not exceed that time. Watch for, wait for, listen to your audience and its reaction. Wait for silence before launching into your main theme. You must command, so stand and speak with authority.

That is why, for all the extremes of their political views, Enoch Powell and Tony Benn are two of the most effective public speakers both inside and outside the House of Commons. They can, at their best, electrify audiences as well as Harold Macmillan ever did. They are both masters of the pause, the cadence, the dramatic gesture. I have seen a totally hostile New York audience of British expatriate businessmen booing Tony Benn on his arrival at a lunch – he was Minister of Energy at the time – and giving him a standing ovation by the end of his speech. By contrast, Roy Hattersley's gabble of talk left a similar audience hostile throughout.

Equally I recall one of David Steel's first speeches as president of the Students' Representative Council at Edinburgh University in the early sixties. It was a boisterous time and a rectorial election had got disgracefully out of hand. His call to the student body to behave themselves in oratory which killed off even the most determined hecklers was one of the most impressive performances I can remember. The students were suitably shamed and the whole mood of the occasion immediately changed for the better.

Adjusting your style to your audience is crucial but difficult to achieve, particularly when that audience is not a unified one. During the national coal strike, the British mineworkers' leader, Arthur Scargill, had a large and highly enthusiastic audience among his membership whom he addressed in his own particular demagogic style. Unfortunately for Mr Scargill, he was not just speaking to striking miners but also to a national audience via the newspapers and the television cameras. The great British public did not like what it saw: it was not just the right-wing newspapers that compared his passion-filled, hate-evoking style to that of Hitler. He may have been an effective leader within the National Union of Mineworkers when everything was going his way. That the tide turned against him was largely due to the national hostility that was aroused in the media and the public by his hectoring public utterances.

Conversely, Sir Ian McGregor, at that time chairman of the National Coal Board, was *not* considered to be an effective speaker or performer on television. This was widely believed to have prolonged the strike because the board's case was not put forward with sufficient clarity and toughness.

TIPS ON DELIVERY

- Start slowly, then speed up a little.
- Modulate your voice more than you would in normal conversation.
- Look at the audience.
- Never (unless you are quoting) read from a text. If you need that sort of crutch it will show you need that sort of crutch.
- Use pauses to emphasize your points (you should actually write the word 'pause' into your speech notes to remind yourself).
- Lowering your voice can add as much emphasis as raising it.
- If you are going to use gestures and swing your arm to make a point, remember Harold Macmillan's advice to move the whole arm from the shoulder and not from elbow (or wrist) – a large gesture has a much more powerful effect.
- Personalize your message. Talk from experience. Give examples.
- A good, forceful message is essential to the conclusion.

ANSWERING QUESTIONS FROM THE FLOOR

Most of the points made in chapter 14 about television interviews apply here. In addition you should remember that for you as the speaker there is no such thing as a stupid question. If the audience think the question stupid they will show it. Your job is to treat everyone the same. Always be courteous. Never talk down to your audience.

Take the heat out of an antagonistic question by appearing to agree. If your company has investments in South Africa, for instance, you can say, 'You are absolutely right to ask this question. We all abhor apartheid. But the way forward is to ...'. You will not get anywhere by appearing to say, 'How dare you ask me such an impertinent question!'

It is useful to repeat the question you have just been asked since this gives you time to think before you answer. It also enables the audience to hear the question properly, and gives you a chance to rephrase it slightly to your advantage.

If you want press coverage, issue in advance an *aide memoire* covering your key points. This should be a *brief* one-page document, not a bulging press handout. The latter will only end up in the waste-paper basket.

As with television interviews, the key to good public speaking is sincerity. Laurence Olivier, when asked what was the greatest secret of success in an actor, said, 'Sincerity, sincerity. Once you fake that, you can achieve anything.' That applies both to formal and informal speeches; with the latter it is almost more important, as F. E. Smith underlined when he said of Churchill, 'Winston devoted the best years of his life to preparing his impromptu speeches.'

Finally, if you are on the receiving end of a speech, remember Bertrand Russell's warning: 'To acquire immunity to eloquence is of the utmost importance to the citizens of a democracy'.

Chapter 16
Negotiating Skills

'Never put anything down on paper, my boy, and never trust a man with a small black moustache.'

From Cocktail Time by P. G. Wodehouse

It is a mistake to think that certain problems can be solved by open discussion. Often it merely makes them worse, as I found when I met representatives of Fleet Street and freelance photographers to try to work out how Buckingham Palace press passes should be allocated. From the chair, I would watch differences of opinion and special pleading decline into bitter controversy, even leading to walkouts by some of those concerned. They did not want to negotiate. They just wanted to get their own way.

Anyone can improve their ability to negotiate, either formally or informally, when positions, policies, contracts or treaties have to be finalized. You too can learn how to use levers of all sorts, how to bargain, how to horsetrade. The key is always to watch out for what might go wrong: the downside.

This includes watching *your own* downside and being alert to when your influence is on the wane or otherwise being eroded. There is little to be gained, when received opinion is firmly against you, in wasting time on those whose ears are closed. Then you should start looking for a new job, a new target on whom to practise your skills, a new world to conquer. In other words, if you, a mature guru in your fifties, find doors closing in front of you and your telephone calls going unanswered, go gracefully. Don't cling.

There are three basic types of negotiator:

1 The hard type, who plays his hand as if it were a constant battle to win.
2 The soft type, who gives and takes, always seeking a compromise.
3 The negotiator who conducts the whole process in terms of seeking mutual gain for both sides. This is the approach that I encourage you to follow, or at least present yourself as following, even though you are Type 1 underneath.

THE TEN QUALITIES OF A GOOD NEGOTIATOR

You should develop the following aptitudes:

1 Know how to assess the opposition and anticipate its plans, needs, fallback positions and determination.
2 Know how to assess the opposition's strengths and weaknesses and its allies. Who really are the most important participants in the negotiation?
3 Know how to stress the advantages to the opposition of a given course of action and how to play down the benefits to yourself.
4 Know how to get the timing right. Do not reveal your own views too early. Let the opposition present its case, then move in.
5 As an extension to this, know how to play the 'creative use of silence' card. In a crucial discussion if you do not talk the other person has to. At the Foreign Office we used to say that the best diplomat was someone who thought twice before saying nothing. Silence is even better than asking questions if the mood is right; it is always a hard argument to counter. Your opponent will give away his thoughts, approach, opinions, strategy. Talk less; learn more. There is a weight

in silence, a great value in an interval in presenting your argument, an influential thoughtfulness in a pause. 'He has occasional flashes of silence that make his conversation perfectly delightful,' said Sydney Smith of Macaulay.

6 An ability to bluff, short of having it called.

7 A skilful use of the threat of a breakdown in negotiations (but always avoiding it in the end). This tactic can usually only be used once, although some unions and management seem to threaten it all the time.

8 Know how to use side issues to take the heat off or to distract attention; know when to back off and when to put the pressure on.

9 Know how to use psychological pressures. Remember the American equivalent of Balliol's 'effortless superiority' characteristic. John F. Kennedy called it 'grace under pressure'. Lesser mortals are fascinated by achievements such as making people listen to you without raising your voice or otherwise demanding to be heard.

10 Know how to constantly question your opponent's position when you are under attack.

When I was the Middle East desk officer in the Foreign Office in the late sixties and early seventies, Henry Kissinger was a negotiator *par excellence*. He possessed all these qualities. Having established himself as an international relations and defence expert, he was first appointed in 1969 as President Nixon's assistant responsible for national security. Four years later, as Secretary of State, he negotiated the ceasefire between the USA and North Vietnam, an achievement for which he was awarded the Nobel Peace Prize.

I saw at first hand how, as negotiator and arbitrator, Kissinger always had the art of reconciling, or seeming to reconcile, irreconcilable differences. During times of crisis his knack of finding a solution, a skill which always went down well with the public, created an image of him as an extremely influential crisis manager. He even escaped being sullied by his association with Nixon. He was a great believer in thinking the unthinkable and realized, in dealing with matters of peace or war, that it was frequently the case that 'if you want things to stay the same, then things have to change'.

BLOCKING

'One does not find men keen on going to certain death,' wrote Machiavelli, and sometimes you will find it is necessary to nip a foolhardy proposed course of action in the bud. When I was in the Foreign Office George Brown came up with a new idea for a British initiative to solve the problems of the Middle East. The distinguished Under-Secretary Anthony (now Sir Anthony) Parsons exclaimed, 'My goodness, that would be a very courageous decision for you to take, Minister.' End of initiative!

Faced with a similar situation in a negotiation, you can resort to one of a number of commonplace phrases that are excellent openers in a blocking move:

'In present financial circumstances (and I need not detain you with all the detail), Mr Chief Executive, it is impossible to contemplate . . .'

'Since it is my duty to warn you of possible threats to your political position, Secretary of State, do you really think it wise . . .'

'The rate of unemployment, Minister, will not allow . . .'

'The inflationary spiral, fellow directors, means that the unavoidably bitter consequences . . .'

'While we must play our part if economies are to be achieved, as you, Mr Chief Executive, will be first to recognize . . .'

'If you are ready for the inevitable drop in profit margins and the resulting outcry from shareholders at the AGM, we certainly can do as you suggest . . .'

'If you are prepared to see increased levels of untreated sewage pumped into rivers, then further economies could be found . . .' (this is a real example, experienced by Michael Heseltine when a Cabinet Minister)

More desperate are the following lines of argument (you are running short of macro-influences if you have to use them), but they crop up in commercial and political life a dozen times a day:

'There is a large body of opinion against this . . .' (and I am part of it)

'The people will not stand for . . .' (for 'people' read also 'workforce' or 'shareholders')

'Future generations will condemn . . .' or, suggesting your inter-locutor may be bent on looking for a new job, 'If you are really looking for a new challenge and are not afraid of the consequences . . .'

Finally, always beware when others say 'There is no alternative' or 'This course of action is unavoidable.'

These are standard committee room phrases. Let us look now at how to deal with committees and their ilk.

Chapter 17
Committee Manipulation

Meetings are indispensable when you don't want to do anything.
J. K. Galbraith

Most people believe that meetings by and large are a waste of time – taking minutes and wasting hours, as the old saying goes. The majority of British executives I know argue that they spend at least half their time in meetings, both formal and *ad hoc*. Some are indeed irrelevant. But meetings happen and they can be used. We may not want to go to them, but we certainly do not want to be left out.

We have meetings for lots of reasons. We hold them because we want to share information or find out what's going on; because we can't take a decision on our own; because we don't want to take a decision on our own; because we want to shelve the matter; because we (all) want to be there when a decision is taken.

In both amicable and confrontational meetings and committees we should aim to hold centre stage when we want to; make an impact and keep our presence felt all the time, even when we are not doing the talking; avoid being ignored or interrupted; neutralize people who try to dominate or intimidate by eliciting their true intentions; keep the meetings both productive and focused on what we want.

If all this sounds rather flippant to you, take care. Many strange devices are put to use daily, along with the more accepted methods of committee work such as genuinely trying to achieve a compromise, careful preparatory work, good briefing papers, trying to avoid unnecessary clashes and keeping to the agenda, all designed to make a meeting useful and to the point, if that is what you want . . .

There are ten apparently cynical but, I can assure you, deadly serious, devious tactics to help you manipulate committees:

1 Make sure all decisions are taken out of committee. In my experience this happens in most boardrooms where there is a powerful chairman. The last thing he will want is a serious debate which might result in things not going his way.

2 Make sure that the membership is properly loaded. This is well appreciated by companies who appoint non-executive directors to sit on their boards. They know, for example, the fact that a man born to a great name or holding an impressive title or office may 'communicate' more influence than he actually has. They consequently choose him in order to manipulate him.

3 Ensure the committee is the right size. It is no new thought that the productivity of a board of directors is in inverse proportion to the number of members (see point 1 above).

4 Persuade the chairman in advance. Always agree with him in public.

5 If you cannot, it may in the longer term be possible to get rid of the chairman.

6 Fill up most of the agenda with trivia. We all know that time spent on a subject must be in inverse proportion to its importance. This is a very serious tactic indeed.

7 Ensure that the most important item is the last on the agenda, to be discussed just before lunch.

8 Watch the clock closely. Ensure that there are only three minutes to deal with the last item.

9 If in difficulty, try the boredom game by speaking in a low voice so that only those whom you want to hear can do so. It adds confusion and irritation which buys time. *Reader's Digest* once advised: 'Keep your temper. Do not quarrel with an angry person, but give him a soft answer. It is commanded

by the Holy Writ and, furthermore, it makes him madder than anything else you could say.'

10 Make absolutely sure you have the last word over what the minutes say. Lead off with: 'Let me summarize what we have agreed' or 'This is what we have decided.' This, at a more developed level, is known as 'marginal drafting'. It is a peculiar skill much used by company secretaries and civil servants, and can only be discerned by the most painstaking who have microscope and searchlight to hand. Few people read minutes. Few people challenge them. Even fewer remember what was actually agreed.

If you still feel that all this is rather fanciful and people don't really behave this way, you are wrong. A British government booklet, *Guidance on the Exercise of the Presidency*, prepared for the UK presidency of the EEC in 1985 and later leaked to the press, included these gems on how to manipulate meetings:

> The UK's objective may be to delay a decision (e.g. until after the UK Presidency). As long as the UK is not isolated, the simplest device will be for the chairman to let delegations ramble on.

> Provided that agreement is not actually staring him in the face, he may be able to conclude that a number of new issues have been raised which require consideration in capitals and reflection by the Commission.

> When the day comes to resume the discussion meetings can then be cancelled because another group needs the meeting room ... and so on.

It even suggests one very useful piece of discreet collusion:

> It is not uncommon for the national delegation to take an extreme position at one end of the spectrum, leaving the Presidency scope for an apparently even-handed compromise which is actually highly acceptable to the national delegation.

There is obviously scope for British diplomacy yet.

OUT-OF-COMMITTEEMANSHIP

Amid all this drivel [in committee] the useful men present, if there are any, exchange little notes that read, 'Lunch with me tomorrow – we'll fix it then.'

C. Northcote Parkinson

Committeemanship is really only an important tool if you have already failed by other means. Failed, that is, to do anything other than ensure that your meeting or committee only rubber-stamps your decision which has already been fixed in the anteroom, the club or over a good lunch well before the meeting itself. A good committee fixer is a potential big guy. A good out-of-committee man, however, wins hands down. He knows his allies and opponents and encourages or neutralizes them in advance as required. He will get an ally to ask the all-important questions, to urge delay, to pick an argument, to be aggressive or conciliatory. He knows the precise psychological moment to say nothing at all. He is also astute in recognizing these skills in others.

Discretion, the wisdom of operating behind closed doors and hiding your light under any handy bushel, is a necessary guard against being accused of 'too clever by halfmanship'. The latter is a difficult reputation to live down. The most successful committee and out-of-committee men hardly ever open their mouths in public but are second to none in terms of pop-go-the-weasel words in antechamber ears.

There was one pre-eminent nineteenth-century British example of such a discreet power behind the figurehead. Prince Albert, Queen Victoria's Consort, had not only an influence on a country but on an entire age. Many aspects of so-called Victorian values stemmed from his German, melded with British, tastes. As Prince Consort, a title granted him in 1857, he took a close interest in the affairs of his adopted country and campaigned for improvements in the arts, education and science. He worked through his political and social contacts, who would then go off to Cabinet or committee to see things through. 'Dear Albert' undoubtedly exerted a great deal of direct political influence over Victoria which not unnaturally attracted a certain amount of mistrust. But because he was intelligently content with the reality of authority without seeking its formal trappings, a rare attribute which is shared by few, his position was seldom challenged. He acted on the principle of merging his own existence with that of his wife, with the paradoxical result that he was effectively though not apparently a decision-maker without peer.

Now while Albert was an excellent out-of-committee man, he was also an excellent committee man. The one does not rule out the other. He set up numerous commissions on a great variety of subjects, knowing when to influence round the table and when in the whispering corridors of power.

DISCUSSION PAPERS

I know one powerful and influential diplomat who always gets his way in casual discussions, in plenaries and in committees, but who loses out on his written material because reason, logic and presentational skills seem to desert him as soon as he puts pen to paper. He cannot produce a discussion paper without overwriting, overexplaining and taking ten pages where one would suffice. The rules are brevity, clarity and a good layout which catches the eye and focuses the reader's attention on the main points. Think how a BBC newsreader does it – give the headlines; fill in the story; summarize at the end.

Rule 30

At the start of a committee meeting distribute a single sheet of A4 setting out your main points. Even those who have not had time to read the committee working papers will read this.

Dean Acheson used to say that a memorandum is not written to inform the reader but to protect the writer. Memoranda should always be read with this in mind.

These then are some of the skills you can actually learn – for interviews, speaking in public, negotiating, manipulating committees – to help you on your way. You have spent years of effort studying for professional qualifications or working for promotion. How much more effective it would all have been (or will be) if you had set aside a little time to work not just on academic or technical matters but on your presentation of yourself. Let us now look at how the professionals in the field do it.

Part Five

Helpers

Chapter 18
Friends and Allies

A shrewd prince should choose wise men for his government, allowing only those the freedom to speak the truth to him.

Machiavelli

You need help, both personal or professional. You cannot do everything on your own. You also need allies and back-up, a well-chosen team, as a source of information, support and advice.

Machiavelli, as usual, had something to say on the subject:

The first opinion that is formed of a ruler's intelligence is based on the quality of the men he has around him. Where they are competent and loyal, he can always be considered wise, because he has been able to recognize their competence and to keep them loyal. But when they are otherwise, the prince is always open to adverse criticism; because his first mistake has been in the choice of his ministers.

Think how many managing directors are hampered because of whom they have in their outer office. Your staff are an image of you as seen by the outside world. If they are flawed or rude or inefficient, that becomes your reflection too.

Advisers come in various forms:

1 The informal: family; friends; casual acquaintances.
2 The formal: immediate staff; professional agents – lawyers, accountants, tax advisers, etc.; peers and other colleagues.
3 Mentors: gurus and personal mandarins, *éminences grises* and possibly spiritual advisers; yes-men, courtiers and courtesans; kitchen cabinet.

4 Paid professionals: image makers; press officers and PR people; lobbyists.

Setting aside the first group – it is up to you to decide how much your family and friends intrude or contribute – it is, first of all, essential to have your own personal, formal, paid 'cabinet' in top-class working order. The rules about staff are simple. First, get to know your immediate staff and your deputies and what motivates them. Second, get to know your deputies' deputies. They are, after all, the most likely successors. Third, give your staff a fine reputation. It works wonders for you and for them. In this context, one of the most honest and quietly determined men I have ever worked for was a former Private Secretary to the Queen. As such he was *de facto* if not *de jure* head of Her Majesty's working household (the actual head of the royal household is the Lord Chamberlain). He was always immensely loyal to those who worked under him and invincible in defence of their reputation. He never looked for scape-goats, although he could be extremely tough with transgressors in private.

We all have specialist advisers: our doctor, banker, lawyer, accountant, cleric. We are influenced by them both because we perceive them as having skills and judgement and because of the reassurance they offer. We think of them as 'good' or 'bad' according to how they please us on both counts. Doctor X may be first class technically, but is brusque and appears heartless, and therefore his advice may be ignored or the patient may seek out another doctor. By contrast, I know of a very distinguished obstetrician whose qualifications and skills are only matched by the great reassurance (much more than mere bedside manner) he gives to his patients. Not only is his judgement wise but it sounds wise. His waiting room is never empty. What goes for obstetricians goes for tax accountants and lawyers in the birth, health and death of business and political figures everywhere.

But remember, the cost of professional advice does not necessarily relate to the value of that advice. We have all come across cases of doctors, accountants and lawyers, particularly lawyers, who move sharply up the scale when submitting their fees. A big bill does not necessarily mean high-quality service. Free advice can be far from worthless.

Rule 31

Watch your peer group. Keep them happy.

Third in this informal series of advisers comes your peer group. They are often your best allies. They can help you with your critical thinking and bring outside influence to bear on your decision-taking. However, it is worth bearing in mind that those who stand back to back with you could be getting ready for a duel to the death.

Some people appear to go out of their way to shun allies or antagonize them, yet in the long run they often achieve much through the sheer strength of their personality. Lord Mountbatten is often accused of arrogance and of ignoring his peer group on the lines of 'I strove with none for none was worth my strife.' In fact, although he had considerable formal military authority during a long and distinguished career, and although he did ruffle many an establishment feather, it was through his contacts and relationships, both royal and political, that his influence lay. His solution to India's problems during partition owed as much to his personality as to his power as viceroy. As a famous name he was always guaranteed publicity for his views, which he was never afraid to air, even when the subject matter was beyond his legitimate jurisdiction. His success made him one of the twentieth century's great fixers and crisis managers.

In contemporary British politics there are several notable loners – Ted Heath, Margaret Thatcher, David Owen. Their problem, as Ted Heath found, is that when they trip they are likely to fall with never a helping hand put out to save them. It is not only in politics that this happens. Daily in the City and in society as a whole great men and women fall largely because they shunned allies and relied totally on themselves. The ex-chairman of Guinness, 'Deadly' Ernest

Saunders, springs to mind as an example, although in his case other
factors were also at work. Some loners make it, but many do not.

> ### Rule 32
>
> **Make sure you have, and people know you
> have, friends and allies.**

Chapter 19
Mentors

A prince who is not himself wise cannot be well advised unless he happens to put himself in the hands of one individual who looks after his affairs and is an extremely shrewd man.

Machiavelli

Friends, family, companions, advisers, professional staff, consultants, and the best of these are gurus. There are quite a few gurus around. We find them in the third group of less formal advisers. They are generally unpaid, secure in their own intellectual position, rising above mere financial gain. Many people in positions of authority have and listen to their guru, feeding off his (gurus are mainly male) wise and not-so-wise advice. Gurus think deep thoughts, and, slowly and with deliberation, utter these self-same thoughts 'all gilt about and well-expressed'. But beware: they are usually, particularly if of the bearded, loin-clothed, mystic variety, just a touch unworldly. There is no special quality that invests a man with the guru's mantle: as usual, he is a guru only if his disciple perceives him to be. He only remains one as long as his client needs him, as an addict needs a drug.

One man who is often labelled a guru by the popular press is the distinguished South African writer and thinker Laurens van der Post, who has acted as mentor to both Prime Minister Thatcher *and* the Prince of Wales. By their own admission he has had influence over them, helping them to think problems through and to understand more about basic human nature.

There are notable gurus in the financial and banking worlds, where certain men are vested with an influence well beyond their own apparent, financially retained status. There is a whole raft of

'Wall Street investment newsletter' gurus – Harry Schultz, Howard Ruff, Joseph E. Granville and others – each of whom has a following of many thousands of share-owning Americans who find that the advice they give, even after the 1987 stock market collapse, allow them consistently to out perform establishment Wall Street advice On that basis, have a guru any time.

THE *ÉMINENCE GRISE*

> A man entrusted with the task of government must never think of himself, but of the prince, and must never concern himself with anything except the prince's affairs. To keep his minister up to the mark the prince, on his side, must be considerate towards him, must pay him honour, enrich him, put him in his debt, share with him both honours and responsibilities.
>
> *Machiavelli*

Distinguishing a guru from a grey eminence in your group of informal advisers is tricky. The latter is a touch more sombre, more calculating, more sinister, more interested in exercising influence than a guru is. Named after Cardinal Richelieu's grey-robed private secretary and *alter ego* Père Joseph, *éminences grises* can have an established place in society and therefore are, perhaps, more influential. They may also have some institutional position: barrister, lawyer, investment adviser, political analyst, academic. The essence of their role is that they exercise what influence they have on both groups (companies, governments, etc) and individuals, indirectly, unofficially, and even clandestinely, in matters and at a level often beyond their nominal authority. They are a sort of one-person establishment. They may be classified as mere mentors or as confidants. Everyone, even the most self-assured, needs either a guru or an *éminence grise* in his life.

Pat Caddell is not a name to conjure with outside the United States and not much of one inside either. Yet he was a professional aide to numerous presidential hopefuls from George McGovern in 1972 to Jimmy Carter in 1976 (his only success story), then on to the disgraced Gary Hart and Senator Joe Biden. Caddell had a great persuasiveness with candidates due to his anti-establishment approach, advocating the bypassing of party activists to appeal via television directly to the electorate. Unfortunately either the candidates or Caddell always seemed to choose unwisely. It was the latter who drafted much of the famous plagiarized speeches that brought about Biden's downfall.

One famous British *éminence grise* was the military correspondent to *The Times*, Basil Liddell Hart. He became such an expert on the German army during the period between the wars that the German army itself became much influenced by his ideas on strategy when it was restructured under Hitler. In 1937 this archetypal 'thinking' soldier (a rare but special breed) became an unofficial adviser to Leslie Hore-Belisha, the British War Minister. As such he was widely resented by formal military circles, as much for the degree of influence he was perceived to have as for his attacks on conventional military theory. Liddell Hart had only intermittent influence on the top officials of the British army and government, due to his inability to penetrate the prevailing conservatism of British military strategy. His experience during that period bears out the oft-quoted assertion that generals are always fighting the last war. His influence was often greater away from both kitchen-cabinetdom and the European theatre: Israeli generals, for example, in the aftermath of the Six-Day War, paid tribute to his tactical theory of striking quickly at weak enemy positions, methods that they themselves employed to great effect.

A contemporary *éminence grise* is that ubiquitous legal mind Sir David Napley, who is never averse to taking on a difficult or unpopular client. I spoke on a platform with him once, to a group of newspaper editors, and his dry wisdom was immediately apparent. Though some see a sinister aspect to his approach and style, it is merely his logical, if cold, professional clarity that causes unease in those who do not know him.

The guru and the *éminence grise* both have their place in shadowing, keeping ahead of, or providing alternative sources of influence for the decision-taker. The danger is that when they become too powerful, as they sometimes do, they replace or overrule democratic and established methods of policy-making in any large organization. Too much of that and the whole structure can crumble. Which is why the one-man adviser is always suspect.

YES-MEN, COURTIERS AND COURTESANS

> There is one mistake which princes can only with difficulty avoid making if they are not extremely prudent or do not choose their ministers well. I am referring to flatterers, who swarm in the courts ... it is difficult for them not to fall victim to this plague.
>
> *Machiavelli*

This is a category, usually pejoratively described, at the bottom end of the influence scale. They are sycophants, courtiers, whisperers in the corridors and the antechambers of power. When they work or come together in groups, they can form the loose-knit kitchen cabinets of the great – feared or despised, effective or, more usually, only reputed to be.

> Rule 33
>
> **White knights and black knights are all the same in the dark.**

The first concern of such people is that, while ability is both important and valuable, the *appearance* of things is crucial. Toadies and sycophants must dissimulate their true feelings, find out what their own particular target decision-taker wants and then cater to that want. This is how they survive, flattering adulators that they are, buying in influence in a not very wholesome way. It means subordinating themselves, working on the craven assumption that subordinates never know better than their supervisors. Such fawning also means keeping in with the right people and being all things to all men. Interpersonal relationships and the skills in this direction thus become ends in themselves. Other objectives take third place.

Such a situation usually develops when the target decision-taker has become a victim of his own success. He believes in his divine right to rule and to do no wrong, and is helped in this by such yes-men who tell him only what he wants to know. The latter are less, even, than the gophers of life (see p. 39), but are more dangerous, particularly if the man at the top likes to bully and sees contrary arguments or criticism, no matter how constructive, put to him by underlings as outright opposition which must be crushed. Needless to say, leadership in that sort of organization needs very careful handling.

One way to deal with it is to educate people to appreciate the need for feedback and criticism, and to point out (if you dare) that sycophants make bad advisers and that anyone who relies solely on them for advice is destined for a fall. Some civil servants I have known have been courtiers, pretending to weigh the facts but always coming out with the 'acceptable' answer in order to cover themselves and to ensure their own survival. Such people will never make good leaders even if the chance comes their way.

Rightly or wrongly a number of politicians in Britain, particularly under a very determined 'prince' like Mrs Thatcher, are considered too close to yes-men for the redder-blooded members of the Conservative Party (who are ridiculously branded as 'wets'). That was one reason vouchsafed for Mr John Selwyn Gummer's appointment as party chairman; and some find Mr Cecil Parkinson of the same ilk – a man born to please more than to act. Critics say that the reappointment in early 1988 of the emollient Robin Leigh-Pemberton as Governor of the Bank of England similarly underscores the subservience of the Bank to Whitehall. Leigh-Pemberton's detractors argue that he lacks the authority and intellectual force of his predecessors, that he is a political yes-man put there to keep the Bank quietly in line with government policies.

KITCHEN CABINETS

Men ... who count most ... should be known to associate with seriously minded persons whom everybody esteems as prudent men. For nothing indicates more plainly what a man is than the company he keeps.

Machiavelli

In any business the real threat to the pattern of official responsibility is the kitchen cabinet whose members have, or are perceived to have, influence outside the main stream of the decision-taking process. The good news is that kitchen cabinets, existing by their very nature as centres of intrigue and ambition, seldom last.

Kitchen cabinets are most obvious in government. No serious head of state is without one since they provide an alternative, and perhaps more loyal, source of advice. But they also exist in many other types of organization. Heads of multinational companies are just as likely to have them on their payroll as presidents and prime ministers.

Kitchen cabinets sometimes really are quite near the kitchens of the powerful. There is every evidence to show that Mrs Reagan wielded enormous influence over her husband, particularly in his less decisive periods and especially over the choice of White House staffers. Robert Maxwell, with his many and varied press and publishing interests, believes in having a personal staff – as much a personal cabinet as kitchen cabinet. But the role is the same. His present chief-of-staff is Peter Jay, the former British Ambassador to Washington, who operates with other hunchmen, including the much moved Mike Molloy, ex-editor of the *Mirror* and editor-in-chief of Mirror Group newspapers. Captain Maxwell's latest recruit to his inner sanctum is an ex-assistant private secretary to the Prince of Wales, Humphrey Mews. Some see these and others in Maxwell's outer office as his cabinet; some describe them as mere gophers for their boss's temperamental whim. But at their best they have more authority than many in the Maxwell empire who appear to have greater institutional status.

The Cabinet Office Think Tank, headed by Lord Rothschild over the period 1970–74, was an institutionalized kitchen cabinet, an elite commando unit, set up to attack the stodgy Civil Service decision-making process. Rothschild was the supreme man of influence. He knew the best methods of persuasion, even to the extent of getting his bright young team coached by his friend the actress Dame Peggy Ashcroft so that they could sway the most hardened minister or civil servant. It worked for a while, then Rothschild left and the Civil Service swept back in over the remains.

Prime Minister Margaret Thatcher has also institutionalized her kitchen cabinet. As well as advice coming to her on the Civil Service and party net, she has her No. 10 Policy Unit, headed by the Welshman Brian Griffiths and staffed by people both from within the Civil Service and from outside – including some from the management consultants McKinsey. These individuals are in a risky profession, as anyone who has watched the fortunes of political advisers in the television series *Yes, Minister* knows. The Establishment does not like or trust them. They have, in consequence, to be very good or very devious to succeed. Weaker members of the species soon give up and leave, or are 'bought' by the Civil Service, which, with more knowledge and resources to dispose of, keeps them happily occupied with trivia. Mrs Thatcher appears to keep the balance very well. She has always had a high regard for the two or three civil servants closest to her, in whom, for a politician of her decided views, she always places a considerable degree of trust. Her former private secretaries – Kenneth Stowe, Clive Whitmore, Robin Butler (now all knighted) – and her current ones – Nigel Wicks and, especially, Charles Powell – have all had a remarkable degree of access to and influence over her. The attempt will always be made to give any leader loyal and committed advice, separate from that proffered by the state leviathan. The kitchen cabinet will always be there.

But what happens behind the scenes is usually reflected, sooner or later, on the front stage. That is where those others – the image-makers, press officers and PR executives – come into their own.

Chapter 20
Paid Professionals

IMAGE MAKERS

Nothing succeeds like reputation.

John Huston

The best way of describing the influential person as image-maker is to give some contemporary examples. In a presidency like Ronald Reagan's, where the chief executive is a detached figurehead, and, in his case, known to be unconcerned with detail, the role of Michael Deaver, until his resignation and downfall, was a crucial one. In Washington, a city where conflicting lobbies are the order of the day, Deaver ruled pre-eminent in terms of confidant and image-maker. To him everything had to be 'mediagenic'. Some argue, rightly in my opinion, that almost single-handedly he created a president out of a B-movie actor. As someone said when Reagan went to China, it was all arranged by Deaver so that Reagan, would-be world statesman, 'could be photographed on a wall'. Deaver's particular relationship was with and through the First Lady, Nancy Reagan. The strength of this relationship meant that his later tarnished image as devious ex-White House influence peddler in no way affected matters behind the scenes. After all, it was he, more than any other, who had created, polished and boosted the presidential image, through an uncanny ability to read and understand his man. He knew how Reagan would react in any given situation and used this to the President's, rather than his own, best advantage. Thus, as *Time* said (August 1984), 'for all his personal influence,

Deaver chooses to behave more like a steward of the presidential image than a shaper of public policy. He is the master of the household, the Lord High Chamberlain of the White House.' Deaver adopted a strategy which others of great influence have used throughout the centuries, and that was to 'hide' the President – that is, when you have a flawed front man, you have to choose very carefully when and how to expose him to the media and to the nation.

In similar vein, personal style, presentation and way of talking are crucial for image-makers like Tim Bell, Frank Lowe, Maurice Saatchi and Sir Gordon Reece. They have no obvious axe to grind except how to be persuasive on behalf of their clients. People sometimes criticize them for not having their own ideas or policies, suggesting that they are perpetual Vicars of Bray. Not so. Of course they have their own opinions. What they are hired for, however, is their skill in presentation, their influence over others in relation to whatever they are hired to project.

How do you become a good image-maker? Step one is to be sure of your own image, to be precise, self-motivated and effortlessly superior without being arrogant.

Rule 34

Match your image of yourself to how others see you. Keep in touch with their reality.

Step two is to look at what is wanted. Does the person you want to influence prefer the clean-cut, mid-Atlantic look or the horn-rimmed, thoughtful-academic type? As Oscar Wilde said, 'A well-tied tie is the first serious step in life.' You have to make your own assessment.

Then you can turn to dealing with your target's own image. Get to know his bearing, style of dressing, speech patterns, behaviour under stress, interview skills, negotiating abilities, and so on, and, without necessarily changing your own image, match yourself to his image and to what he most appreciates. Do not try to upstage him. Be a touch more conservative in dress and style rather than the reverse. Avoid claiming high status or reputation for yourself lest you get it wrong. Once that has happened it is hard to undo.

Remember, as step three, to play as required on both the vanity of self-important men/women and the vanity of important men-/women. The latter often have just as much as the former, since modesty, like immunity to flattery, seldom walks hand in hand with greatness. Caution makes me fail to mention contemporary examples; from the recent past, however, both Mountbatten and Field-Marshal Montgomery spring easily to mind.

There are two distinct types of image-maker. At the most basic these are the press officer, who puts out the personal or party line, and the public relations (PR) person, whose skills principally lie in working out what the best line should be.

PRESS OFFICERS AND PR PEOPLE

Public relations is organized lying.

Attributed to Harold Wilson

Individuals, groups, companies and political parties all feel they ought to employ press spokesmen and public relations advisers not just to bolster their image but to get that image right. After all, their competitors do.

Some great people have no need for such spokesmen or advisers. Others, with some of the most gifted among them, are poor communicators, do not wish to speak publicly or need to be protected from the media, and therefore require someone to act for them or interpret what they say and think.

There is another category of great figure who gets it wrong in front of the television cameras and reporters with their pencils and notepads at the ready. President Ford was one such – he made his press secretary work overtime. My erstwhile colleague, the aptly named Larry Speakes, long-time press secretary to President Reagan, was adept at appearing shortly after a presidental press conference to say, 'What the President meant to say when he said X was Y' and so on. The President was celebrated for getting names and occupations wrong – calling the President of Egypt the President of Israel on one occasion, and misnaming the Princess of Wales twice in one speech at a White House banquet. Even Larry couldn't do much about that, though his moderated, low-key way of speaking tended to defuse many of the worst gaffes. It is obviously deliberate policy to use such spokesmen. His successor, Marvin Fitzwater, is low-key to the point of hardly being there at all.

In his book *The Making of the President*, 1960 Theodore H. White, a confidant of the Kennedys, showed how he played a great part in building up the Kennedy image or myth. Americans have long been doing it – making or selling the President. It is only relatively recently that there has been a similar move in Britain to sell the Prime Minister or would-be Prime Minister – influencing the electorate not with promises or policies but with personalities. It was, for instance, as late as 1959 that the Tories became the first British political party to use an advertising agency – Colman, Prentis and Varley. The Labour Party mocked and criticized them for selling themselves like washing powder, but meekly followed suit from 1964 on. In the 1987 general election it reached a peak, with the official Conservative Party employing one agency, Saatchi and Saatchi, but the Prime Minister herself secretly using not only the ex-Saatchi supremo Tim Bell but also the services of the advertising agency Young and Rubicam. All three groups were vying for the privilege of promoting or selling Mrs Thatcher. The same, if much less convoluted process, lay behind the selling of the Labour leader Neil Kinnock. Again it was his personality, concerns and family life that were promoted rather than the policies of the Labour Party. At the end of the day, however, several studies and surveys suggested that less than 2 per cent of voters said that they were influenced by all the press advertising over which so many had agonized. We shall return to the subject of advertising later.

Press officers and PR people work in three totally distinct types of situation:

1 When they are promoting something successful and the media is watching and reporting every action. This might be a new car, a new type of washing powder, or a new cure for some illness.
2 When they are planning a promotion and want the media to take notice. Here they adopt an 'any news is good news' approach. Never mind the content, look at the number of column inches. This can apply to the launch of a new product or perhaps a controversial film where the controversy itself may be deliberately inflated for this very purpose.
3 When something has gone wrong and a damage-limitation strategy is called for. For instance, if there is a radiation leak from a power plant, British Nuclear Fuels will bring all its PR expertise into play.

Many PR exercises and PR people are a complete waste of time. Those who rely heavily on their PR person or company are in constant danger of being exposed. The senior executive, the key influencer and his decision-taker must always be in direct charge of the PR staff, not the other way round. PR people are there to be used. At their best they can do a great deal, particularly in the business world, in terms of promoting a product or a service. In such circumstances, however, a PR consultant – i.e. someone who will advise you as to how *you* should do it – is often very much more cost effective. A few common-sense tips and ideas from a consultant and any good executive can do the job. The media are much more likely to listen to a hard-working decision-taking top executive or managing director than a paid, smooth-tongued spokesperson. The exception to this rule is when the top figure is irremediably boring or otherwise ill-equipped to project a case, as when Ian MacGregor was in charge of the National Coal Board during the miners' strike. It took some time and courage to bring in Michael Eaton to act as public spokesman in his place. He was next down the executive line and knew how to project himself and the required message. He was senior enough and free to act and speak without having to refer back; authoritative and perceived to be informed; and reasonably glib and credible in the battle with Arthur Scargill.

So much for the press secretaries and PR executives. But, increasingly importantly, there are also lobbyists. What are they and how do they do it?

LOBBYISTS

There is no such thing as a free lunch.

City saying

Lobbying suggests something vaguely improper. Normally it is perfectly democratic with individuals employed by companies or other interests and given a brief to watch the development of actual or potential legislation and monitor any parliamentary business that might affect their clients; or to effect changes to the client's benefit; or to explain the case to those who matter – MPs, civil servants, and, if possible, to members of the government direct. The lobbyist is a professional influent – generally a hidden persuader who will shun the limelight when he can.

'Knowing someone' matters a lot in most societies. The lobbyist (not to be confused with the Lobby, which means those discreet journalists who are meant to report the affairs of Parliament and Government without disclosing their sources) is the political relations arm of any organization, the contacts-fixer, the oiler of the interlocking wheels of industry and government.

Lobbyists are the up-front, hard-nosed bit of the PR game, the free-dinners people, the flatterers, the purveyors of freebies and junkets, from bunches of roses for a wife to free air tickets to anywhere. If they are good, they know more about what is really going on than any politician or mere civil servant.

They normally concentrate on single issues, using all the influence tools to enable them to manipulate the existing system to best advantage. They are exponents of the 'who you know is all that matters' argument. They will put the right people in touch with the right people. They are door openers, interlocutors, dressed in a patina of respectability, manipulating campaigns, from letters to MPs to mass whispering in ever-ready ears. As one Washington lobbyist remarked, 'We are conduits through which clashing attitudes reach decision-takers.' That is a generous way of putting it.

Unlike politicians, who are working for political goals, the lobbyist is in the business of making money, of being paid for doing what this book is all about. Employed by the big-name companies like Shell or IBM, they are specialists in getting to know what the politicians are thinking, as well as in helping them with that thinking. Many powerful industrialists, some of whom are politicians in their own right, do their own lobbying. Usually they are more effective, since political animals of any authority want to speak to the top rather than, as is the case with the PR people, with a mere mouthpiece. Lobbyists may also represent trade associations and other groups who have an interest in keeping the government, Parliament and legislation in line. They inhabit the no-man's-land between industry and politics.

In Britain, where lobbying is a fast-growing business, there are an increasing number of lobby organizations which carry some authority. Among the best known is GJW (Gifford, Jeger and Weeks, when they set their operation up, had respectively been working as advisers to David Steel, James Callaghan and Ted Heath, and you can't get more nicely balanced than that). They probably have a fair effect in certain specific areas or on single issues in which their clients have little experience of Whitehall or Westminster. As a mark of how closely they mesh with the whole PR and advertising industry, GJW is now owned by Lowe, Howard-Spink, a firm which knows its market well, which is why ex-civil servants as well as politicians are on its payroll. In that regard GJW are closer to their American counterparts than many of their rivals, with a frequent role in lobbying against or for major industrial takeovers. They and their ilk fought over Westland, the Guinness–Distillers battle and

Boeing when it was locked in conflict with GEC over a $1 billion airborne radar contract in 1987. They can do this sort of thing very effectively yet relatively anonymously, with their names scarcely ever mentioned in public.

Sir Trevor Lloyd-Hughes, who was formerly press secretary to Harold Wilson, is another who believes strongly in a confidential relationship between himself and his client. Even to admit who his clients are, he believes, would diminish his effectiveness, and his clients themselves would also be unhappy for the relationship to be widely known about.

Lobbyists, by definition, thus prefer to be unacknowledged, except by their client, aiming to do the job without being noticed. Information about their success rate is consequently hard to come by since the best lobbyists realize that boasting about what they do would make their target decision-takers much more difficult to reach in the future.

A current problem arises from this desire for secrecy as many major lobbying firms have MPs on their payroll. This is where conflicts of interest begin and is why many legislators urge the need for a registrar of lobbyists, particularly if 'success fees' are payable if a campaign works. Some good lobbyists argue that such fees ask for trouble by encouraging bribery or other corrupt methods of influencing events.

Direct lobbying is a high-profile activity in the UK by organizations such as the CBI, the Institute of Directors and Aims of Industry. But experts in the lobbying game claim that direct access by such interest groups to the seat of power is now largely confined to window-dressing meetings. The government of Mrs Thatcher certainly prefers informal discussions with industries of its own choosing and reacts against more blatant lobbying exercises. An exception are the political in-house lobbies such as the Centre for Policy Studies – the most pro-Thatcherite of all – which provides think-tank and background briefing to its captive audience rather like the Fabian Society used to do to some sections of the Labour Party.

There are many other types of lobbyist – mainly 'one causers', some of whom we discussed in chapter 11. These are people with

no power but who know how to build up and wield influence. And
they have their successes. They get films banned, they stiffen the
laws on drunken driving, they defeat plans that would destroy a
wildlife reserve or natural beauty spot.

Lobbying is much more intense in the United States than in
Western Europe, where it is still in its infancy, and the American
media scrutiny is much more rigorous. In America lobbying often
equals something nasty; it is known pejoratively as 'peddling
influence'. There were, at the last count, at least 10,000 people
involved in lobbying the Washington, DC, alone, so it must be
effective and profitable. But they have to be registered.

In March 1986 *Time* wrote:

> At tax-writing time, the Washington lobbyists line up by the hun-
> dreds in the corridor outside the House Ways and Means Committee
> room, ever vigilant against the attempts of lawmakers to close their
> prized loopholes. Over near the House and Senate chambers, Con-
> gressmen must run a gauntlet of lobbyists who sometimes express
> their views on legislation by pointing their thumbs up or down.

Time went on to argue that while there have been lobbyists in
Washington for as long as there have been lobbies, never before
have they been so brazen. What used to a somewhat shady and
disreputable trade has burst into the open with determined respectability. Tempted by staggering fees, for many a period of public
service has become a mere internship for a lucrative career as a
'special interests' consultant. Sometimes they go too far, as Mr Lyn
Nofziger, a former political director at the White House did: he was
found guilty of illegal lobbying in violation of conflict-of-interest
laws.

Lobbyists sometimes seem to cancel one another out. But they
also have the power to obstruct and their effect can be corrosive.
However the private individual does occasionally benefit from
special lobbying and not all lobbyists are evil, devious or without
scruple. Righteous advocacy can sometimes obviate devious lobbying.

Chapter 21
Electioneering

Saying the right things to the right people; saying different – but not inconsistent – things to people in different types of constituency; saying different – but not inconsistent – things to different sorts of people within constituencies.

Recommendations to aspiring SDP candidates (1986)

As a footnote here, among the professionals we must number those who are trying to influence because they are running for elected office. This book does not pretend to be a campaign runner's *vade mecum*. But how to make friends and influence voters when you are standing for election or trying to be selected for any position which requires people to choose you over others is simple provided you follow certain guidelines.

- Be everywhere.
- Set yourself a minimum target of sixty handshakes a day (times ten, of course, when on the political campaign trail).
- Smile and look confident. You don't have to kiss babies. (If you have halitosis or acne it becomes mandatory not to.)
- Don't waste time on hostile voters. Press on fast.
- Follow up any expressions of interest with a personal letter (or what appears to be a personal letter).
- Produce a pad and be seen to take notes of your voters' or constituents' complaints.
- Come across as an uncommon man/woman of common principles.
- Watch your private life does not trip you up.
- Close gates and don't step on flowerbeds.

As a student of political candidates for office and their techniques,

Influence

I am constantly amazed at how things like dress, hairstyle, perceived attention span (looking over the shoulder of the person to whom you are meant to be talking to spot more important people in the room is a sure vote loser – we can all admit to doing this sometimes) and other presentational matters which *can* be rectified seldom are. As in so many areas, such little niceties win out over policies again and again.

Now let us turn to look at how groups in society attempt to influence each other and how the process is in many ways very similar to what we have already considered.

Part Six

Groups and Super-Groups

Chapter 22
Old and New Elites

In modern times, it is only by the power of association that men of any calling exercise their due influence in the community.

Elihu Root

All professions are conspiracies against the laity.

George Bernard Shaw

Just as individuals can exert influence, so can groups in any society. They employ the same methods; they need the same skills. Groups come in various forms. Sometimes, as with the Bloomsbury Group or various action groups, their influence is very much greater than the sum of their constituent parts. They include formalized structures, pressure groups, industries, power clusters, casual alliances (formed to deal, perhaps, with one single issue) and lobbies. Consider some of the best known of them: big business, the City/Wall Street, the Establishment, the church, the unions, established political parties, clubs and travel associations, the Civil Service, the professions, the armed services, the media (see Part Seven), and what Americans call PAGs – political action groups – such as the arms manufacturers, the farming/agricultural lobby, the conservationists, and even Animal Liberation Front, Greenpeace, Gay Lib, Militant Tendency, CND and the Young Conservatives. They all have their effect in a way. In the end many of these groups believe that the group that always wins is the Establishment. Let us begin by looking at that.

THE ESTABLISHMENT REVISITED

A wise prince must devise ways by which his citizens are always dependent on him and his authority.

Machiavelli

Machiavelli's 'device' in the case of Britain (and most other 'democracies') is often held to be the Establishment. It was defined in the 1950s by the British journalist Henry Fairlie as 'the whole matrix of official and social relations within which power is exercised' – in other words, that body of individuals, acting consciously or unconsciously, who, though not necessarily holding any official posts, have great effect on a country's national policy. The *Oxford English Dictionary* adds that it achieves this 'by virtue of its traditional superiority, and the use especially of tacit understanding and a common mode of speech, and having as a general interest the maintenance of the *status quo*.'

Does it exist? Does it matter if it exists? Who is in it?

So far as the last question goes, the Establishment is sometimes thought to be the Bureaucracy (but is this anything other than the Civil Service?), the Old-Boy Network or the Meritocracy (often called 'the rich, the wise' – sometimes 'the able' – 'and the well born').

However, the answer to the first question, and hence to the other two, is that in present-day society the Establishment does not exist except in some people's minds. It is, if anything, a creation that has been developed by the media and fuelled by the great public, who feel that there must be an élite who should be getting together to fix things and therefore ought to have attention paid to it. Even if it did exist, the Civil Service leviathan would drug it with the valium of its own sheer size.

There are, of course, professional establishments in every country and groups in every society, as the film producer David Puttnam found when he tried to take on the entrenched might of traditional Hollywood. I recall him saying that the battles of principle that he was obliged to fight allowed him no time to produce films, and that the attitudes in Hollywood, where greed is the main creed and talent is intimidated, would lead to its collapse in the end. 'But sadly, not yet,' he added drily.

A much better way of thinking about things is to envisage a number of robber barons – businessmen, financiers and politicians – constantly fighting over the national booty and only uniting in order to force more out of the kitty than is there to be fought over. When they unite in such a manner I refer to them as the 'Closetists'.

THE CLOSETISTS

> One man proceeds with circumspection, another impetuously; one uses violence, another stratagem; one man goes about things patiently, another does the opposite; and yet everyone, for all this diversity of method, can reach his objective.
>
> *Machiavelli*

The global Establishment is more or less a figment of the popular imagination, but the Closetists, an ever-changing strategic pattern of groups of unimotivationalists, are always around. They

(a) deny their existence as a group,
(b) prove this by frequently not acting as a group,
(c) but equally frequently act in unison,
(d) have no organization,
(e) but frequently act as if they had,
(f) have no membership list,
(g) but all know the other members of their 'club',
(h) which of course does not exist (see (a) above).

Commonly confused as being separate parts of the Establishment, usually by those on the extremes of the political spectrum, they are not; but they are hydra-headed. They include such diverse bodies as:

– the Pinstripe League (cells to be found in the City, round St James's and along Pall Mall), such as the CBI, Aims of Industry, the Institute of Directors, the Institute of Bankers, the Finance Houses Association and so on, who appear to be separate but act as one when confronted by a serious threat;

- the Association of Latterday Telepundits, now largely found around Sir Robin Day at the Garrick, the Fleet Street antecedents of this group having died off or otherwise gone into self-induced liquidation – the El Vino's syndrome. We will come back to them in chapter 27 under the heading of 'Opinion Formers' – those who attempt to tell the great British public what it should be concerned about and what is the media hobbyhorse of the month;

- the Union of Permanent Under-Secretaries (who deny to the death that they exist), which is the closest thing there is to an Establishment;

- the Guild of Younger Turks, who are the bright young, future has-beens of tomorrow. They are the youthful fogies of both left and right. They read the *Spectator*, the *New Statesman*, or some such and care passionately about things – at least from time to time.

Generally speaking such Closetists carry more credibility and weight than, for example, the much written and talked about but largely moribund groups of tired and emotional parliamentary backbenchers. The latter, despite certain assertions and ambitions to the contrary, tend to be equated with 'Trafalgar Square on Sundays' demonstrators in terms of serious political relevance. Who in government, except if there is a tricky vote or by-election coming up, ever pays any real attention to the views and opinions of committees of backbench MPs? When, for example, did the 1922 Committee last influence anything?

Note: Closetists, as with legitimate pressure groups, always use extraneous influences in their support: e.g. 'Unless you introduce the Care and Protection for Furry Gremlins Bill, Minister, I fear that the National Campaign for the Abolition of Ministerial Perks, or NATCAMP, has threatened to demonstrate every time your official Rover turns up at your taxpayer-supplied house to take your wife shopping.' Even the hardest-nosed minister is vulnerable to the domestic lobby.

Chapter 23
Conspiracy Theory

Men are so simple, and so much creatures of circumstance, that the deceiver will always find someone ready to be deceived.

Machiavelli

On the other hand, he also wrote: 'There are countless obstacles in the path of a conspirator.'

Conspiracy theories emerge in society from time to time. What is the real truth; what is the true reality? For many people, groups and, indeed, nations there is always a plot, a conspiracy going on, the hidden hand being manipulated by some sinister faction either within the organization or without. The far left, the far right, the capitalists, the Establishment, press barons, communists, Jews, Masons, Opus Dei, the City, Militant Tendency, Gays, moist Liberals, etc. All the world wants a good old sinister plot. A conspiracy is a first-line, bread-and-butter defence mechanism for any politician on the run, any petty tyrant, US president or ayatollah whose politics are going awry. (Can you imagine the press barons actually working together in happy oligarchy?) Well, cast aside most of that rubbish, but husband two small grains of truth: events tend to be stage-managed and natural allies band together.

Managing directors and chief executives get together, when there is a need, to present in order to persuade. The media coordinator, lobbyist, press secretary or PR person works off-stage as playwright, prompter, orchestrator, make-up artist and stage manager. Then the actor comes on stage to say his or her lines. At the end of the show the actor takes his bows, the cheering or the boos. The real conspirator exits unnoticed by the stage door and heads for the telephone.

People love conspiracies and plots. That is what much of popular entertainment thrives on – television drama especially. Things must never be what they seem; latent Mafia must lurk round every corner of life. Thus the fascination with cover-ups on espionage matters. The Peter Wright *Spycatcher* story conjures up tantalizing memories of Burgess, MacLean, Philby and Blunt, and creates images of right-wing establishment plots to overthrow the very democratically overthrowable Prime Minister, Harold Wilson. Wilson may have had his faults. Having worked in the Cabinet Office over part of the period in question, I believe that such a plot simply did not exist, though doubtless some individuals did get as far as talking about 'wouldn't it be nice if . . .'.

A similar story concerns the newspaper dragon Cecil King who reportedly discussed various plots to 'bring sense to the British people' with figures like Mountbatten and others. Such people often feel they have power when all they have is their names in the newspapers on a fairly regular basis. In practice they end up not even having influence, unlike, for example, Tiny Rowlands who undoubtedly wields considerable political influence, particularly in parts of Africa, because of his industrial muscle. By contrast, he is shackled in his ownership of the *Observer* – a paper that has often criticized the activities of companies like Lonrho – because of the existence of an independent board that oversees and protects the interests of that newspaper. Constraints, as I said at the very beginning, are always there.

Chapter 24

Government and Civil Servants

Once it is understood that politicians are public relations officers for their publicity-shy bosses, the Civil Service Permanent Secretaries, Parliament and politics become intelligible.

David Frost and Antony Jay

Presuming as we must for the purpose of this book that the government is a target for influence rather than an agent of influence (and I realize, of course, that the government spends huge amounts of time and energy on influencing us), our interest tends to focus on the roles of civil servants and the party machines in politics.

If there is an elite, an establishment, in any ostensibly democratic system, it consists not of ministers and other elected representatives of the people, but of the unelected arm of government, the top civil servants or mandarins. By their very permanence and by the self-selection procedures by which they are appointed, they are inevitably more talented and more knowledgeable than their political masters (coupled with being lofty, enigmatic and sometimes threatening). They are also more experienced with facts and with the machinery of government. They, with their negotiating skills, are the professional oilers of wheels, when they want to be; otherwise they can produce 'a difficulty for every solution', as a former British Home Secretary, Lord Samuel, once complained.

They are able to win the confidence of totally opposing political masters (the last Secretary to the Thatcher Cabinet, Sir Robert Armstrong, was previously Private Secretary to both Edward Heath and Harold Wilson; and Prime Minister Thatcher's Press Secretary,

Bernard Ingham, was previously Press Secretary to the left-wing Labour Minister of Energy Anthony Wedgwood-Benn).

They have more contacts with other decision-takers from their peer group in other walks of life than have any of their supposed political masters. At the same time they almost always avoid any serious critical scrutiny from outside.

They are urbane, detached, sardonic, sceptical and have an ability to manipulate ministers and committees alike. In the civil servant these virtues are seen as vices. How unfair. Their owners are the great and the good, who only occasionally lapse into the sin of following the doctrine of administrative convenience.

They, or rather the top few hundred of the several hundred thousand civil servants in Britain, are the power-pullers of society; the rest are just the cogs and wheels. They are the tyrants of the minister's in-tray, the guardians of the doors and windows through which all political influence must flow. As Lord Armstrong, an ex-head of the Civil Service said, it is a 'self-perpetuating oligarchy, and what better system is there?'

The political stage in Britain is littered with very able people who have tried to bring about a reform of the Civil Service and failed. It can change itself, slowly from within. But when highly talented people like the businessman and current director-general of the Institute of Directors, John (now Sir John) Hoskyns, came in as head of Prime Minister Margaret Thatcher's Policy Unit and tried to introduce new ideas and attitudes, he failed, as did his successor, the distinguished journalist Ferdinand Mount. Though the latter went through periods when his personal influence was profound, in terms of changing the structure and sheer inertia of the Civil Service, he would, I believe, claim to have been largely defeated.

This is not to argue that aspiring influents should become civil servants, at least not if they wish to see quick results for their efforts. Having been a civil servant – or rather a diplomat – for over twenty years, I now realize with joy the differences in the private sector. In the latter the influent can have a much more speedy effect, can act rather than react, can see his policies quickly put into practice (or, of course, rejected), rather than having to wait for endless scrutiny by official and committee right up the heavily layered pyramid of rank, authority and obfuscation. Of course, there are companies whose management structure mimics if not rivals the civil and government system in terms of sloth and fear of taking any real decisions, but in the highly competitive 'real' world of commerce, where the warning motto is 'A square stone gathers lots of moss', they are unlikely to survive for long.

Chapter 25
Big Business

Persuading people to like your company and your product is a sound marketing ploy. It can, however, be a lengthy process. I have always been impressed by the spot-on view of Bob Worcester, the chairman of MORI, who argues that corporate images 'improve as slowly as glaciers move, but can be destroyed overnight'. He goes on, 'The building of a corporate image is like planting asparagus – you should have started three years ago.'

Thus we cannot complain about those nice guys at the Mobil Oil Corporation who for years have been funding British television programme makers by giving the American people the gems of the largely British made 'Masterpiece Theatre'. Why do they do it? Mobil is not, it would be the first to agree, a quiet, cosy little operation. Few can rival it in its aggressive pursuit and public defence of its worldwide interests, with its 'issue' or 'advocacy' type of advertising. It appears, unlike some big corporations which avoid controversy, to like to go out and pick a fight.

But Mobil's main aim, with support from 'Masterpiece Theatre' and culture generally, is to show goodwill and make people like it. This is what is known as 'side influence'. If you love them you will buy their product. Thus sponsorship in all its forms, from opera to football, caters to a huge market constituency. This is the fun side of the coin. Such good works seek to identify Mobil not with oil but with enjoyment: 'We love you, Mobil. Thanks a million.'

As with Mobil, so with most big business. Corporations want to be liked, to be seen as caring and compassionate and, with all the Machiavellian skills at their disposal, they often succeed. They sponsor in order to appear to be good citizens – what some of the big banks call their social balance sheet – giving back whence they have taken (though usually limited to an amount that is less than 1 per cent of pre-tax profits).

Take another example: the industrialist Armand Hammer, who made his first million dollars while still a student at medical school, went to Russia in 1921 as a volunteer to help alleviate the disease and famine that bedevilled that stricken country. He ended up, with Lenin's personal encouragement, fostering trade contacts between the USA and the Soviet Union by operating mining and manufacturing concessions. In 1930 he returned to America with a considerable fortune and a large collection of former Romanov art treasures. Many years later, in 1973, as the dynamic head of the Occidental Oil Corporation, he used his Russian contacts and experience to sign a multi-million dollar barter agreement with the Soviet Union, while as a connoisseur of Russian politics and art he also did much to improve the governmental and cultural relations between Russia and the USA.

His influence is, of course, as much 'personal' as 'big business' and is undoubtedly huge. Though an unabashed capitalist, Hammer has proved to be a man the Soviets seem to trust and respect. This has enabled him to cross ideological barriers and meet the Russians on amicable terms, an accomplishment which, until recently, few American or Western politicians have achieved (or indeed valued). Some admirers argue that his influence is due to his personal knowledge and understanding of the Russian people, his deep interest in Russian culture and his straightforward and uncomplicated business dealings. Others hold that every success he has in this field is, like all big business, due to one primal factor – his money – and that he has bought his reputation and with it the influence he has.

As with Hammer and Mobil so with many of the giant multinationals that now span the globe. They are often the bogeymen of the left, and sometimes with justice, as when ITT tried to play political powerbroker in South America or when the Firestone Rubber Company used to run the independent state of Liberia. IBM, General Motors and countless others have stood accused of exerting 'undue' influence, mainly in the political field, lobbying for legislation in their interests. And what is so wrong with that? Their influence is very much 'due' in terms of their national and international status and their contributions to both national and world economy. In any case, the influence of big business is almost certainly less than it is usually perceived to be, since the governments of nation states tend to lean over backwards *not* to be influenced by such multinationals in pursuit of their individual goals. But, in return, many top industrialists and their companies actually *want* to improve the lot of the countries they operate in. They want to be philanthropic. Much sport and culture across the globe would collapse overnight without the sponsorship that is mutually beneficial to donor, recipient and to the public audience at large.

Continuing with the example of the oil companies (and they have provided a unique example of the most effective influence techniques at work on a global scale for the past many decades), they have certain specific objectives and even more specific targets. In terms of their North Sea interests – taxation, competition policy, pricing, bids to develop new fields and so on – they will want to: influence the government of the day; more especially the Department of Energy; more especially its ministerial oil team; more especially that group's senior civil servants; more especially the chief of its planning staff.

Their effectiveness will depend on:

- Their status vis-à-vis the government and how this is balanced by the interests of other sections of the economy, relations with Arab and American oil companies and so on.
- The relative strengths of will of the companies and the ministerial team. How sure is each side of its case? How determined is it? Is there a crack in the unity of one side or the other? One company may be less determined to fight the new revenue taxes than another because the former wants to be better positioned as a goody-good boy when it comes to new allocations of North Sea fields. Is, on the other hand, the Minister of Energy going to have his position undermined because his permanent secretary, unbeknown to him, is about to retire, having been secretly

offered a position on the Board of Grease (Dallas) Inc.?

– Their perception of each other. It is usually different from the reality. Some groups deemed to be influential frequently suffer from the well-known reverse-influence syndrome. (God help the Minister if the Friends of the Clean Seabed come rushing to his side.) More commonly, a reputation for being influential often imparts just that quality: the great, the wise and the believed-to-be-good are always around.

– Whether they are actually willing to use their resources and fallback positions. They do not always want to flash them in front of the opposition. Possession of the wherewithal under a dirty raincoat is very different from a full frontal on the min-isterial position. If you are going to wield the big stick you have to be pretty certain that it is going to work, for there is no industrial grouping quite so pathetic as one that has failed. The world knows the folly of spitting into the wind without an umbrella to hand.

There are many other examples of monopolistic or oligopolistic power, like those who lobbied hard for legislation to make yellow reflective numberplates compulsory on the rear of all British regis-tered cars. They were, purely coincidentally, the sole suppliers of the reflective material required.

Chapter 26
Nation to Nation

A prince also wins prestige for being a true friend or a true enemy ... revealing himself without any reservation in favour of one side against another. This policy is always more advantageous than neutrality.

Machiavelli

Having examined the influences that individuals and groups in society have, let us look at how influence relationships work at the highest level – between nations, or what might be termed supergroups. The techniques and skills needed are more or less identical.

First, some basic facts:

- Most international influences are outside the control of any one nation.
- The overwhelming power of the superstates is irrelevant for most practical purposes (remember the power–influence spectrum). Great nations are often as unsuccessful in getting their own way as the small nations. Think of the Soviet Union and Afghanistan, or the United States and Nicaragua or Iran, or Israel, or Libya or South Korea.
- Too much 'power' may be counter-productive. Client states feel threatened and tend to break away.
- Powers and superpowers buy influence in the form of government aid programmes. These may buy influence but they do not necessarily buy friends.
- Much of what has been said about interpersonal/intergroup

influence relationships, e.g. timing, mechanisms, perceptions, image-making and so on, applies equally on the international stage.

British influence, for example, depends on what value judgements are made in other individual countries overseas about the United Kingdom and its perceived national characteristics. Power, such as it was, has gone. Britannia certainly does not rule the waves (though occasionally she flexes her muscles, as over the Falklands). But still you will hear the phrase that Britain 'still counts for something on the world stage'. Why, where and how? If Britain still has influence, it is based on: (a) tangibles, such as her economic position, the City, diplomatic and political pressure, military and defence mechanisms, North Sea oil, and aid and technical assistance programmes; and (b) intangibles, such as the monarchy, the colonial legacy (and relics of empire), democratic institutions (the mother of Parliaments and all that), 'fair play' (the 'friendly British bobby' syndrome), the world-wide use of English (and the BBC World Service, the British Council, etc.). The fact that Americans spoke English was, to Bismarck, one of the greatest factors in nineteenth-century international relations.

Taken as a whole, the list may look impressive. But if examined closely, it soon becomes apparent that it is all done by mirrors: there are a large number of reflections of a small object, but the object itself still remains small. The danger is that it may only be the smallness that others notice.

In some ways, however, the British, or individual Britons, can be highly influential on the international stage without setting out to be so. The Beatles wanted only to produce exciting music. They ended up influencing international pop culture over a generation in matters of dress, style and behaviour. Similarly the Princess of Wales has, inadvertently, brought about great changes in fashion around the world, not by setting out to do so but by popular example.

Overall the cultural influence that Britain has is probably more valuable than many commentators suggest. Talleyrand's famous exhortation to French ambassadors about to take up their missions,

'Make them love France!', is hardly something one can imagine the present Foreign Secretary Geoffrey Howe saying, since the phrase 'British culture' tends to stir up visions of Morris dancing.

British officialdom dislikes self-advertisement. Sir Anthony Parsons, a former British Ambassador to the UN and subsequently Mrs Thatcher's own foreign affairs guru, in a lecture in 1984, spelled this particular factor out with simple clarity:

> If you are thoroughly familiar with someone else's language and literature, if you know and love his country, its cities, its arts, its people, you will be instinctively disposed, all other things being equal, to buy goods from him rather than from a less well-known and well-liked source; to support him actively when you consider him to be right and to avoid punishing him too fiercely when you regard him as being in the wrong.

American influence rests on a similar raft of tangibles and intangibles, although sadly, in large parts of the globe, Machiavelli's dictum, 'Men's hatreds generally spring from fear or envy', applies. Add to that another of Machiavelli's remarks, that 'It is much safer to be feared than to be loved when you have to choose between the two', and you have a neat summary of the American condition.

Americans would rather be loved than feared, but successive Washington administrations often appear to have taken to heart a third piece of Machiavellian advice: 'It is a good notion at times to pretend to be a fool.' Unfortunately they are not always pretending. Slow to anger and swift to forgive they may be, but they tend to think that the man on the white horse will win in the end, which is why they often lose out in the influence game.

Like British influence, American influence may look impressive, only more so, but client states do not really like big brothers, benevolent or not. Real American influence works best behind the scenes. It is not the aggressively imperialist, Voice of America, Yankee, CIA posturing, but *The Quiet American* approach that bears fruit in the end.

DIPLOMACY

For *our* country, wrong is right.

Machiavelli

According to David Frost, diplomacy is the art of letting somebody else have your way. Diplomacy really consists of saying and doing something very nasty without appearing to. It is soft-core rather than hard-core lobbying at international level, employing the subtle word and the medium of the cocktail party to best effect. At least until harsh words are necessary.

Diplomats are professional negotiators and reporters of the international scene. With the ease of international travel leading to frequent summitry, it is sometimes mistakenly thought that the days of the diplomat are numbered. Not so. The success or failure of a summit meeting has been influenced and decided by career diplomats long before the summit takes place. Diplomats are not found to the left of the cut-off point on the power–influence spectrum. That, along with the constant need for secrecy about real intentions, is why they are often criticized for inactivity. Behind the scenes things are very different.

A supreme example of all these qualities was found in the consummate skills of the French diplomat Talleyrand, which brought him a long reign of influence under successive regimes. He was, in turn, bishop, president of the revolutionary Constituent Assembly, and Foreign Minister, a position he retained after Napoleon's coup d'état, which Talleyrand himself largely engineered. He used his diplomatic talents to consolidate Napoleon's victories, but later, believing that the emperor was not acting in the national interest (and hoping to improve his own position), he entered into treasonable relationships both with Tsar Alexander and with Metternich. He played a brilliant but secret double game to bring about Napoleon's deposition, and, as Louis XVIII's foreign minister at the Congress of Vienna, he then embarked on a damage-limitation exercise to safeguard French interests. Fifteen years later he was appointed ambassador to Britain bearing Louis Philippe's credentials.

Talleyrand's long-term importance lay in his astonishing cunning and freedom from the ethical constraints which inhibit other, lesser mortals – and even today's career diplomats. They, of course, moral to a man or woman, are hindered in embarking on any neo-Talleyrandish ploys by the mere fact of the efficiency of modern communications. The modern diplomat is all too often thought of as a well-paid, well-dressed and well-educated postman, with the marionette string tightly controlling his every *nuance démarche*. In fact, diplomacy is far from dead, and great skills of persuasion, gentle and often less so, are still employed in the embassies, chanceries and legations of the modern world.

One of the bluntest weapons of international influence is propaganda, which relies heavily on the skilful use of sweeping generalization, slogans and unqualified assertions. It is a matter of getting individuals, groups or nations to believe that they share common interests with you when in fact they do not.

In the Western world propaganda is usually recognized for what it is and is weakened by competing sources of information and the democratic process. More subtle forms of it face us every day, courtesy of the advertising and PR industries of the world. It is just a large framed version of media manipulation and, through the media, the attempted manipulation of men's minds. It still exists in great measure in some parts of Eastern Europe – Romania, where I spent several years in the embassy, is a sad example of it continuing into absurdity through its horrific adulation and personality cult of President Nicolae Ceaușescu. It exists too in parts of the Third World and, tragically, in a negative form through state-imposed censorship (the reverse of the coin as it were) in the Republic of South Africa.

In the end, as the arch propagandist of the Third Reich, Dr Goebbels, was to discover, propaganda, although it may be a means whereby the state apparatus can propagate what it wants to say, cannot control what people think.

Part Seven

The Public and the Media

Chapter 27
The Voice of the People

The populace is by nature fickle; it is easy to persuade them of
something, but difficult to confirm them in the persuasion.

Machiavelli

The influence of any group, as of any individual, is to do with what
its peers, allies or opponents think of it. It also to some extent
depends on the view of the public at large. Often that is irrelevant,
but sometimes it matters very much indeed.

Public opinion is often believed to be one of the greatest of all
macro-influences. This is not so. Public opinion is neither balanced
nor logical and is seldom consistent, though it may have an effect
none the less. It is summed up by George Burns's remark, 'Too bad
all the people who know how to run the country are busy driving
taxi cabs and cutting hair.' The fact is that businessmen, politicians
and other leaders of society recognize the importance of public
opinion only if that opinion is codified and an AGM or a general
election is looming. As Voltaire said, 'Once the people begin to
reason, all is lost.' Public opinion is moulded by the media, but the
media often reflect or are moulded by public opinion.

The art lies not so much in manipulating public opinion, which
may be beyond the skills of even the most influential, as in using it
if it is blowing in your direction and even if it is blowing against
you.

The latter can be achieved by the use of deft phrases like 'We all
know how unreliable public opinion polls are' or 'The swing is
coming hard in our direction' or 'They'll come round to our way of

thinking in the end', or simply quote Charles James Fox, 'I will not take the word of the people from a few demagogues any more than I will take the word of God from a few priests.'

There are, however, ways of manipulating public opinion. People expect their leaders to be well informed, fluent and persuasive. Do not disappoint them. Remember that there are only two groups in society: them and us. If you have or can get public opinion on your side, capitalize on it while it lasts. But watch out for overkill, the kiss of death that can turn whizzkids into waskids overnight. The worlds of business, entertainment and politics are littered with the corpses of those who once had everything, plus public opinion, going for them. Western society and the Western media in particular like creating great figures and then sniping at them until they fall.

OPINION POLLS

Some princes flourish one day and come to grief the next, without appearing to have changed in character or any other way. This I believe arises, first, for the reasons discussed at length earlier on, namely, that those princes who are utterly dependent on fortune come to grief when their fortune changes. I also believe that the one who adapts his policy to the time prospers.

Machiavelli

Never mind whether opinion polls are representative of what people think in general – indeed, it is not worth worrying about whether they give an accurate reflection of anything. The main questions are, first, do they matter? and, second, do they themselves exert any influence?

We are all familiar with the following sort of report: 'In a sample survey of left-handed DIY enthusiasts, 83 per cent said they would prefer screw threads to run the other way, 5 per cent said they didn't know and the rest used nails.' So? Informative? Instructive?

There are constant arguments as to how influential opinion polls are in themselves. Some countries ban them in the final run-up to an election as it is often claimed that people want to back a winning horse. Politicians, despite what they may say when their opponents have a 15 point lead, really do think opinion polls are important. Like them or not, they belong in the armoury of any modern political influence system. Their minor siblings are various sorts of consumer polls of the 'Do you prefer Stork to butter' variety. These certainly influence manufacturers, sales managers, investors, advertisers and even the consumers themselves because they have been specifically framed so to do.

> Rule 35
>
> **Treat opinion polls with caution. They can be useful. It depends on how you use them.**

OPINION-FORMERS

Nothing is more suitable to restrain an excited crowd than respect for some man of gravity and standing who in person confronts them.
Machiavelli

One way to change things – and most companies are only too well aware of this – is to go for those who most affect public opinion or the required segment of public opinion. Perceived wisdom and gravitas in a man or woman can have a massive effect. An opinion-former is someone who, through the public expression or dissemination of his views and his advocacy of causes, has actually influenced public opinion as well as the opinions of lesser or would-be opinion formers. Groups in society therefore pay an inordinate amount of attention to them. In our age they tend to be concentrated in the media, particularly in television.

While in the Diplomatic Service, at Buckingham Palace and now in industry, I have always argued that one should go for the media person who counts. The editor of Britain's ITN, the self-effacing David Nicholas, despite the fact that he almost never goes front of camera, has wielded huge influence in his behind-the-scenes scrutiny and control over what is considered news and the standards that the half-hour 'News at Ten' (watched by an eleven million-odd audience) and its sister programme adhere to. Along with his colleague and friend, Sir Alastair Burnet, he has maintained a consistently high quality, seldom descending to the level of the popular press in Britain with its daily diet of sensationalized trivia.

Nicholas has been branded the 'lifeforce' of ITN for almost a quarter of a century. What he decides should be presented and how Burnet presents it deeply affect the opinions of a multitude. Their teamship, their influence on each other and on their colleagues provide hope in depressing times for Britain's media. There are other examples: the 'Today' programme on Radio 4 and the formidable 'World This Weekend' are listened to by many of the major decision-takers in the country.

As an example of an influential non-media person, Lord Denning, for twenty years jurist and Master of the Rolls, has long moulded public opinion as the champion of the rights of the individual. His favourite subjects were victims of bureaucracy and deserted wives. This made him, via the media, popular with the public, though his preference for the pursuit of justice over precedent made him a controversial figure in legal circles. His popularity, backed by his pre-eminent use of short, simple sentences when making a case, ensured a wide and influential audience. It meant that all his decisions, opinions and utterings, both in and out of court, obtained a wide hearing. He was adept at making the most of this, not for his own but for a larger benefit.

There is another respect in which Denning is a very good example of how to maximize influence. No sooner was he elevated to the House of Lords as a Lord of Appeal in Ordinary than he accepted the job of Master of the Rolls – a hierarchical *demotion* – because he knew that his consequent influence would be all the greater. Many more cases would come his way for a decision, and for one to go in his favour he would only need to carry one colleague with him, since appeals are heard by only three judges in the Court of Appeal, as opposed to five in the House of Lords. Moreover, as Master of the

Rolls he could ensure that all the most important cases came to his court – a splendid example of working the system.

Chapter 28
The Fourth Estate

Men always dislike enterprises where the snags are evident.

Machiavelli

The media use and are used. They are for ever telling us who has status, who is listened to and who not. So they must, themselves, be influential. Or are they? Consider the following questions:

- Do editorials or major articles in the serious (non-popular) newspapers have any real or lasting effect?
- Do editorials in the (popular) tabloids matter?
- Do radio or television outweigh the print media in terms of changing public opinion?
- Does what appears in the gossip columns have an effect?
- Does the fact that most stories are hyped up to add 'reader interest' matter? (There is an old Fleet Street story about the correspondent who cabled his editor: 'It is difficult to exaggerate the seriousness of the situation here – but I shall do my best.')

There are no simple answers to the above. For instance, people talk a lot about the influence of newspaper proprietors. How great is it? Take, for example, Rupert Murdoch, among the biggest Anglo-American-Australian media barons of all time. He exerts, through the range of newspapers and television stations that he owns, a huge indirect political and social influence in Britain, the United States and in his native Australia. His down-market newspapers have given a new depth to sensation, page-three, yellow journalism with all its social consequences. Yet, unlike Lord Beaverbrook, Murdoch has not obviously attempted to influence governments directly, although all his efforts have gone towards curtailing union power and almost all his newspapers are, unsurprisingly, well to the right on the political spectrum.

If I have one simple conclusion it is that the influence of newspaper stories and comment – and I have been the subject of many over the years – has little effect beyond the day on which the item or the editorial appears, unless a campaign is mounted and sustained over a period of time, and this rarely happens.

As for television, its persuasiveness is widely recognized, as the continuing debate on sex and violence demonstrates. Yet sometimes such influence is accidental, as when a character in the well-known British soap 'East Enders' attempted suicide with an overdose of sleeping pills and hospitals subsequently reported a significant increase in overdose admissions.

In the end there is really only one thing to remember when a would-be influent – be it a person or a group – is exposed to the media: the more publicity you have, the less effective you will be in influencing a specific course of events. And if that publicity is ill-informed, as it will be in the print media, it will be all the more dangerous. 'He will print them out of doubt; for he cares not what he puts in the press,' said Shakespeare in *The Merry Wives of Windsor*. Thus a moderate union leader like Norman Willis will have a much harder time at the negotiating table if he is constantly branded as a moderate. (Remember, however, that a reputation for being influential actually helps you to be influential.) The same is true for groups, say a company or a business. Thus the real extent to which PR forces are employed to influence and manipulate the media should be kept under wraps. That is why 'open' industrial relations negotiations are always harder to conduct. The ill-informed get in on the act; prejudices are catered to; firm stands are transformed into unyielding ones, for fear of appearing weak to those on the sidelines. That is also why 'open' government works badly, since it is difficult to negotiate complicated or subtle issues under a full public gaze.

MANIPULATING THE MEDIA

> He should not deviate from what is good, if that is possible; but he
> should know how to do evil, if that is necessary.
>
> *Machiavelli*

In chapter 20 I describe the work of the would-be media manipulators, press officers and PR executives. But true media manipulation is a rather different category and is usually equated with news management. No one is better at managing news than the media themselves. Except in totalitarian states, the media have no real authority, but their destructive influence is enormous. Few believe that the press in particular, but also radio and television, are merely in the business of purveying information, passive bearers of the flame of truth. Of course they are not. They too are firmly into the business of influencing and persuading.

Individuals, as we have seen, can manipulate the media by, for example, acquiring the skill of appearing to be sincere on television. Groups can go further. Here are ten basic rules for any organization which wants to get its own way with the media:

1 Get the news out in your terms first (but not with press releases – they are 99 per cent waste-paper-basket fodder). Make it interesting and remember the advantage of leaking to a media outlet. Others will feel constrained to follow up the story.

2 Denials seldom work. As we saw in chapter 14, *never* deny an allegation; it will just keep the story running. Do not over-react to small or even medium errors. 'Rise above it, ride it out' is the key. Above all, if you sue you will usually be damned (unless you are Jeffrey Archer). Corrections and apologies come but seldom, and when they do they are never given the same prominence or have the same effect as the original story.

3 Second versions (the 'real' story?) seldom work, particularly if the first version was more exciting. (The bishop wasn't in a brothel; he was visiting a sick aunt.)

4 Put your story out just before the deadline, giving the opposition no chance to deny or contradict it. For example, if you are aiming at a much watched or listened-to programme such as 'The World at One', 12.30 p.m. (as the Foreign Office will tell you – they do it every day) is a good time for making things known for maximum impact.

5 Use embargoes to heighten attention and to give the media time to research the background, but only if that is likely to work in your favour.

6 Guard against the media's 'too good to check' excuse (i.e. a story is too good to check). *Sun* journalists always followed this line when I was Press Secretary. They would not ring in to check an unsubstantiated rumour since it would be denied and they might then be forced to kill the story.

7 Ascertain who is the top media opinion former (i.e. the person who has the most influence among his/her colleagues, if such exists) and concentrate on them. It may not be the editor-in-chief, but rather the city editor or the senior political correspondent.

8 Give them a memorable quote. I once made a comment about a so-called 'royal pundit', stating that 'he spoke neither with knowledge, understanding, nor with any authority on the subject.' It is still used every time his name comes up.

9 Think mediagenic. A good picture to back up a good story always wins over a line that is hard to illustrate.

10 You will never have it all your own way. The media can be stubborn when they want. With a cause behind them there are some journalists who will not be manipulated. One such was Bob Woodward, of the *Washington Post*, who, with Carl Bernstein, uncovered the Watergate scandal. He is quoted as saying: 'I think there must be an adversary situation in any case of investigative reporting. They kept saying we were liars. We had to prove them wrong. The only way we could do it was with solid facts.'

Some final thoughts. The media are unelected and as undemocratic as any other professional interest group. They shape the news by slanting, tailoring and selective reporting. Journalists are supreme champions in the use and misuse of adjectives. They talk about the right of free speech, the necessity of freedom of information, which usually only equals the right of the journalist to say and write what he likes and get away with it. At best the media act as popular orator; at worst they are cheerleaders for lynch mobs, swelling popular causes and expectations to excess, exacerbating and playing on every popular emotion. They act as public prosecutors, accountable to hardly anyone. They are not impartial observers: by their very nature they are partisan in their support for issues and for what they believe people ought to believe.

But we need never fear that the media will be manipulated for perverse reasons for very long with father figures like Charles Wintour, former editor of the *Evening Standard*, or Sir Edward Pickering, the doyen of what was Fleet Street and close adviser to Rupert Murdoch, watching in the wings. If, in private, they deplore some of the press's worst excesses, they are always ready to defend it from wider attack. They are the media gurus, the grey eminences, who matter more than most editors and proprietors put together when the real freedoms of the press are at stake.

Chapter 29
Not-So-Gentle Persuasion

In the ad business, sincerity is a commodity bought and sold like everything else.

Newsweek

It is said that half the money spent on advertising is wasted, but you never know which half. It is also said that doing business without advertising is like winking at a girl in the dark. You know what you are doing, but does she? In fact it all really depends on what else you are doing and how dark it really is. A candle manufacturing company prominently advertised one batch of their product as 'Imperfect – half price'. The advert was, strictly speaking, correct and the Advertising Standards Authority could do nothing about it. The candles had no wicks.

Advertising ranges from massive corporate campaigns – companies projecting themselves to the world at large as prosperous, patriotic and benevolent – to specific advertising which tells you about goods and services that would otherwise be unknown – a car to sell, a department store sale, a church fête. There is also exhortative advertising which advocates Brand X over Brand Y and relies on the cumulative effect of newspaper and television exposure, billposters and so on.

Watch the ads on television; pick up any newspaper; thumb through a batch of women's magazines. Look at the full-page spreads for cosmetics, baby products, soap powders, personal computers, dog food, items relating to intimate personal hygiene. Sit back and think. What do all these do for you? Do you consider yourself to be like some latter-day Pavlovian dog? Are you *really* influenced by all these huge, glossy and very expensive pages? Are we all, producer and consumer alike, victims of some sort of massive con trick? Test yourself on familiar and unfamiliar slogans to see how advertisement-conscious/prone to persuasion you think you are. Why, if most surveys and opinion polls produce figures which purport to show that the vast majority of consumers do not believe in advertising and think that they are seldom if ever influenced in their purchasing decision by advertising, is there so much of it? The answer is: because the consumers are wrong.

The most interesting aspect of advertising so far as this book is concerned is its immense influence on social behaviour and fashion. The desire to ape one's peers is as strong as any motivating force. And advertising caters to that. The *Financial Times* advertising campaign with the slogan 'No *FT* No Comment' is a splendid example of this. The vast majority, even the intelligent, educated minority, likes to be told how to think. To the *FT*'s target audience, the suggestion that without the *FT* they might be ill-informed is distinctly worrying. Result – they go out and buy the *FT*. They are intellectually reassured.

To be effective in advertising, as in everyday influencing, you have got to know about what the profession calls VALS (values and lifestyle), as well as the so-called four Cs (cross-cultural consumer characteristics) which categorize people by social and other criteria and therefore identify the pressures they are under to conform. If a person is in Group X, he needs and can afford Y.

But perhaps the advertisers' target, the consumer, does not actually want or realize he wants what is on offer. All that must change. Advertisers must create a demand or at least awake a dormant need. 'Yes, sir, you really cannot do without this brush for cleaning your green wellies. What? You don't have green wellies? Oh dear. Everybody has green wellies.'

You, as advertiser, must seek to influence, if not your target directly, then your target's spouse, children, neighbours, workmates and so on, to show him that he needs and wants what you have. You may have to make some changes in what you have on offer by altering the style, content, quality, price and so on, just as manufacturers of everything from dog food to washing powders come up with 'new, improved' versions of their product to stimulate demand. Then all you have to do is find the slickest way of presenting your product to give it the widest possible appeal. The principle is the same whether you are marketing consumer goods or a political party. Wherever there is something to sell, be it an object or an idea, advertising will be there.

Envoi

I am not unaware that many. . . hold the opinion that events are controlled by fortune and by God in such a way that the prudence of men cannot modify them, indeed, that men have no influence whatsoever. Because of this, they would conclude that there is no point in sweating over things, but that one should submit to the rulings of chance.

Machiavelli

The renown of great men should always be measured by the means which they have used to acquire it.

La Rochefoucauld

We are all, knowingly and unknowingly, manipulated by a plethora of pressures, habits, micro- and macro-influences. We are bent and moulded by rapidly changing fashion, styles, arguments, personal restraints, by money, by ambition, by success and failure. We are often bound by our own deep, inherited prejudices. Machiavelli consistently argues that half the things we do are due to Fortune; the rest are controlled by ourselves. Not a bad starting point; or finishing point. In any set-piece situation, the muddy waters of intrigue and influence, sullied occasionally by corruption, are the lubricant of any decision-taking machinery. The influential are the cogs. To be influential one has to be perceived to be so. As we have seen, there are some techniques, many of them very small but very important, that can be learned. As Napoleon said, 'The outcome of the greatest events is always determined by a trifle.'

There is a new breed of persuader abroad in the world of business and politics. Inside any organization such individuals are merely known as influential; outside, they are what are sometimes called 'facilitators', men and women who peddle a nebulous blend of access, management, promotion and expansion of any given interest. They act as guides through the decision-making maze of interpersonal relationships, fuzzy establishment peer groups, corporate bodies, societies and the political structure of nation states. They buy up the means for changing public and individual perceptions, steering their clients through political, social and commercial minefields, polishing up the public image of person or cause, buying the media, buying the public, in a race in which, to misquote Gandhi, the longest purse finally wins. Such men and women are the new achievers, PR consultants, government affairs specialists, corporate and public affairs advisers.

Their success is measured in the great and little things of life. If one of them is good at wheeling, dealing and appeasing, he and his fees run as close as a hand in a pocket. The influencer is a hard-nosed operator. He knows, like Count Metternich, that 'gratitude is not an active sentiment in politics. It is a mistake to take account of it'. He keeps his apparent success factor high by never colliding with the impossible, always quietly guiding his target along the road to a conclusion that he himself has long since reached. The prime rule, if you need to hire one, is to check him out first with one simple test of his ability: when he telephones the great and the good in the land, *do they return his call?*

With sublime lack of modesty, Niccolo Machiavelli in dedicating *The Prince* to 'The Magnificent Lorenzo de Medici', wrote:

> Men who are anxious to win the favour of a prince nearly always follow the custom of presenting themselves to him with the possessions they value most, or with things they know especially please him; so we often see princes given horses, weapons, cloth-of-gold, precious stones, and similar ornaments worthy of their high position. Now, I am anxious to offer myself to Your Magnificence with some token of my devotion to you and I have not found among my belongings anything as dear to me or that I value as much as my understanding of the deeds of great men.... I could not give you a more valuable gift than the means of being able in a very short space of time to grasp all that I, over so many years and with so much affiliation and peril, have learned and understood ... and if you read and consider it diligently, you will discover in it my urgent wish that

you reach the eminence that fortune and your other qualities promise you.

A very reasonable aspiration. In the nineteenth century it was said that anything could be achieved by the three levers of lust – drink, women and bribes. There was also something called power. It is much more complex now. Such basic levers have their place even in the last decade of the twentieth century, but in the end it is intellectual nimbleness and subtlety that win the day.

Index